California Mormons

by Sail and Trail

California Mormons

by

Sail and Trail

by

ANNALEONE D. PATTON

Published by
DESERET BOOK COMPANY
Salt Lake City, Utah

Printed by

DESERET NEWS PRESS

In the United States of America

Mormon Contribution to California History
in the Pre-Gold Discovery, Pre-Constitution
Period, and in the First Seven Years of
Statehood.

By

ANNALEONE DAVIS PATTON

I AM ONE

I am only one,
But, still, I am one.
I cannot do everything,
But still I can do something;
And I will not refuse to do
The something that I can do.

—Anonymous

Preface

The purpose of writing this little book is to share information which I have gleaned, over a long period of years, on the contribution of the Church of Jesus Christ of Latter-day Saints to early California history.

The segment of the Mormon migration which came by water to California's shores has been by-passed by many writers of history, particularly by writers of church history. This was a church-sponsored (but not financed) plan to move the Atlantic seaboard members to the "Upper California," which included the Great Basin, where they hoped a new Zion might be established.

These exiled Mormons chartered a cargo ship, the *Brooklyn*, and sailed from New York on February 4, 1846. As far as can be ascertained, it was the first colony of home-seekers with women and children to sail around Cape Horn. The *Brooklyn* Saints were the first Anglo-Americans to come to California by water; the first colony under the United States regime in California; and, except for a hide, the first ship to sail into San Francisco's Golden Gate after the Stars and Stripes had been raised in San Francisco by Captain John B. Montgomery three weeks before.

Caroline A. Joyce, of the *Brooklyn* kept a daily journal during the voyage around the "Horn." The journal also included the first five or six years of her life in San Francisco. It was considered invaluable for the reliability, accuracy, and fullness of historic detail. She entitled her work *Early Annals of California*. This marvelous manuscript mysteriously disappeared at the time of her death. The loss of the document is inexplicable as Mrs. Joyce had discussed the matter of publishing it with her daughter during her final illness.

This first colony of Mormons was almost the gene in

the germ of the American way of life in the pre-gold, pre-constitution days of California. Not only did the Mormons contribute much to California history, as will be shown in the pages that follow, but their farms, orchards, vineyards, and tithing also gave much to the colony at Salt Lake City to make life tenable in its early days.

Reference to Mormon activities in California are frequently buried within a paragraph, or asterisked to footnotes and seldom indexed, except among such historians as Hittell, Bancroft, W. T. Sherman, and others. When writers and researchers began blowing the dust off old manuscripts and books to revitalize the California Story for the Centennial Celebration of 1948-1949-1950, the original facts proved more interesting than fiction or legend.

Of Samuel Brannan much has been written which depicts him as a lovable, reckless person, but he was not representative of the early Mormons, their tenets, nor their beliefs. It is the purpose of this book to bring to light the lesser known history of the 238 passengers of the *Brooklyn* and their contributions to California history.

I wish to express gratitude to Mrs. Helen Bretnor and others at the Bancroft Library who helped me so much with my research. Invaluable aid was also given to me by members of the Berkeley Public Library, the Oakland Library, and the California State Library at Sacramento. I also wish to express deep appreciation to Mrs. J. P. Green of Sacramento for chauffering me to many points of historic interest.

Contents

View of San Francisco, formerly Yerba Buena in 1846-1847.

CHAPTER I

Pacific Pilgrims

When through the deep waters I call thee to go,
The rivers of sorrow shall not thee o'erflow,
For I will be with thee, thy troubles to bless,
And sanctify to thee thy deepest distress.

—Robert Keane

Pandemonium broke loose when shore birds were sighted by the men on watch on the *Brooklyn*, a freight ship, in the late afternoon of July 30th, 1846. The human cargo, 238 exiled Mormon home-seekers, had been brought from their cramped quarters between decks where the overhead was so low that an adult could not stand erect. Weather permitting, the immigrants were brought up to the upper deck for exercise.

In the sunset, sheen on the ocean flashes twinkled like struck steel. "That's the flip and dip of some land huggin' critters—sea lions or porpoises!" the man in the crow's nest yelled to the cheering, shouting crowd. Their goal was in sight.

Captain Richardson, his crew, and the Mormons were anxious to put into port. It had been a long, dreary, six months' voyage from New York. However, the next morning a thick summer fog swathed the *Brooklyn* and her passengers. They lay off the entrance to San Francisco Bay in the pre-dawn blackness awaiting the sunrise and the later clearing of the fog. Captain had been told that San Francisco's summer fogs seldom lasted all day.

The Mormons went below to the big table to sing hymns and have "family prayers." They were too excited to sleep. This would be, perhaps, their last occasion to

sing praise around the all-purpose table. Earlier, when a
terrific storm raged after rounding Cape Horn, Captain
Richardson feared the ship would break up. He opened
a hatch to warn the religionists of their fate. The *Brooklyn*
was pitching and bobbing over mountainous waves and
into cavernous troughs. Above the shriek of the hurricane
he heard the Mormons sing Cowper's famous hymn:

> "God moves in a mysterious way
> His wonders to perform.
> He plants his footsteps in the sea
> And rides upon the storm."

In a voice muffled by unshed tears and fright the
captain said: "It looks like we can't keep afloat much
longer."

"Be of good cheer, Captain. We're not going to sink.
We're to California, wherever it is—God has called us,"
comforted Elder William Glover. "Let's sing Elder John
Taylor's song, 'The Upper California, Oh that's the Place
for Me.'"

The crew had been apprehensive every long league
of the cruise, because they had shipped before the mast
with women aboard, where women had never been before.
There were whispered accounts that wives of missionaries,
and women of adventure had sailed through the Straits
of Magellan, but these Mormon women would be the first
around Cape Horn. It was an evil omen. "Women aboard,
they've brought bad luck. We're under a curse 'til we're
rid of 'em," grumbled the crew.

All was still now, except for wavelets nuzzling the
ship's side and for a cow bellowing for her weaned calf in
the hold.

Captain Richardson had his beard buried in the grimy
almanac. He raised his bushy brows and held a split finger-
nail on a line he was reading. "San Francisco Bay has a
tide every six hours. If this tormented fog lifts before

sunrise, we'll sail in slick as a whistle," he murmured.

The ship's yeoman was writing an entry in the log. "24,000 miles!" he exclaimed. "That's 6,000 miles more than we reckoned on."

"Storms," snorted the captain, who resented any comment as an affront to himself or the ship he loved. "On the Atlantic we were blown almost to the Cape Verde Islands. Then she rounded Cape Horn neatly through the early autumn Antarctic blizzards up to Valparaiso, only to be blown back to Antarctic waters and out to the San Fernandez Islands. Yet she lost neither a man nor a cask of grog. A good ship, a darn good ship!" said the huffy old captain.

The voyage of the *Brooklyn* was, perhaps, the longest continuous sea journey of any religious outcasts in history. The Israelites crossed the Red Sea on their way to Canaan. The Pilgrims of 1620 crossed the Atlantic, a voyage of about 3,000 miles or more, and were on the water sixty-three days. These Pacific Pilgrims (Mormons) crossed the equator on both the Atlantic and Pacific Oceans, went from the icy Antartic to the tropic Hawaiian Islands, and thence to California, a voyage of 24,000 miles. There were 120 Puritan Pilgrims; and Pacific Pilgrims numbered 238 souls. The two groups were alike in many respects. Each group was composed predominately of young people with small children. They had dauntless courage, intrepid daring, matchless faith, and trust in God.

The chartered *Brooklyn* sailed from New York harbor on February 4, 1846. This was not an isolated expedition, but a seagoing segment of the great western migration of the Church of Jesus Christ of Latter-day Saints. The church had moved westward from the moment it had become an organization. From New York, its birthplace, it migrated to Ohio, from Ohio to Missouri, and from Missouri to Illinois where it built a beautiful city, Nauvoo, as headquarters.

After the martyrdom of its founder and leader, Joseph
Smith, persecution became acute. The Council of the
Twelve Apostles is the governing body. In 1845 the Council decided to leave Illinois and prepared for a move
towards the setting sun, somewhere beyond the vacant
prairies over the great Rocky Mountains to establish themselves in the wilderness of *The Upper California*. Their
people had frequently been dispossessed of land and
chattels. They had proselyted among the masses, and many
converts had been recruited from the poor or underpriv-
ileged. As an organization the Church had neither resources nor credit.

The Church Authorities deemed it expedient that its
New England and Atlantic seaboard members, whose fi-
nances were inadequate to buy wagons, teams, and provisions to take them to Nauvoo, Illinois, the starting place,
should pool their money and charter a ship. Orson Pratt
of the Council of the Twelve Apostles went to New York
to help organize the expedition. It was highly publicized
in such church-owned papers as the *Times and Seasons*
(Nauvoo) and *The Millennial Star* (England).

Elder Samuel Brannan, an enthusiastic young printer
of New York, was chosen as leader and authorized to charter a ship. For weeks on end Brannan tramped the water-
fronts of New York and Boston unsuccessfully seeking a
hide drogher. War clouds hovered low. Both the United
States and the Republic of Mexico seemed to be watching
for the other to commit the overt act. Ship owners and skippers would not charter their vessels for a long cruise, when
war might bring government contracts, big profits, and
quick returns. Also, it was difficult to recruit a crew that
would sail with women aboard. Indefatigably, Brannan
persisted until his sincerity and Irish smile won the ear of

---

*Drogher, a Dutch name for a coastal fishing ship—where the catch was
dried aboard—Calif. hides often dried on the ships. (Webster's New Inter-
tional Dic.)

Captain Richardson of the *Brooklyn* and part owner of the 370 ton cargo vessel.

Joyfully Brannan brought his counselors to discuss terms with Richardson. "My price is $1,500 per month, you pay all port charges and your own food." The poverty-stricken young Mormons knew the price was beyond them.

Elder William Glover, Brannan's first counselor, said, dejectedly: "We are a group of two hundred and forty people. One hundred are children, seventy are women, and that leaves only seventy men."

"Fifteen hundred a month is my price. I'm not in this business for my health. The *Brooklyn's* a swift ship. She has no equal, I'm a tellin' you," said Richardson. He loaded each nostril with Lundyfoot snuff as he watched the men walk down the icy, cargo-piled quay. "Hi there!" he called. "If you home seekers are willing to sacrifice your own goods and fill the hold of the *Brooklyn* with some of this plunder piled on the wharves waiting to go to Sandwich Islands (Hawaiian Islands) I might be able to scale down the price to $1200 a month."

The charter was soon signed on Captain Richardson's last terms and a down payment was made. Immediately Captain Richardson hired ship carpenters and began converting the space between the decks into living quarters for the immigrants. A long table was built the entire length of the ship. This was to serve for school, dining, council meetings, "bishop's court," work and sewing, recreation and singing, and Sabbath services. Backless benches were spiked, wedged, and bolted with equal security around the table. Except for berths, there was no other seating. On these benches they sat, fed small children, or knelt at morning and evening for "family prayers." Sleeping cubicles were built on all four sides. Families and relatives usually berthed together.

Many of the Mormons had not met until they boarded the ship. Some had never seen the ocean, none had taken an ocean voyage. Yet, strange to say, there was comparatively little inharmony. The Mormons were to learn before the journey's end the wisdom of building the table, benches, and hard, shelf-like berths so solidly. This low ceiling, restricted walking space, and the cramped quarters were a far cry from the crisp, spacious New England kitchens to which they were accustomed. Brannan, Glover, Pell, Orson Pratt, Captain Richardson, and his first mate worked hard to compile a code for rules of conduct aboard ship. Brannan and his counselors drew up a plan for division of labor for members—for the women there was waiting upon the table, washing dishes, and the teaching of school and singing; for the men there was cleaning and caring for the two cows, pigs, and chickens in the hold. Two Negro cooks were hired. Many men members hired out to Richardson as carpenters and ship fitters, others did stevedore work in storing the cargo in the hold. Loading and conversion of the vessel delayed the sailing date many days.

The women visited loved ones for the last time. They knew that they would never see their dear faces again. California was as far away as the "Isles of the Blessed." Empty handed, but not unskilled, they awaited the sailing date. It took much longer to "rig up" the between decks space as living quarters for the passenger than had been expected. Then a heavy snowstorm came and slowed the stevedoring work on the docks. The homeless Mormon families huddled in cold, crowded, inadequate rooms, or accepted the hospitality of friends or other church members in the city. All rejoiced when Captain Richardson announced that the ship was ready. Then the unexpected happened. The government might stop the *Brooklyn* from sailing to California!

While Brannan was seeking means of securing cargo for the Pacific, he contacted the Postmaster General on the chance that the government might give him a contract to take mail to the Sandwich Islands. The Postmaster General informed him that there was no mail to California and little to the islands. However, he, himself, was interested in the boundless unowned land of California. His duties as a public servant prevented him from going to California, but he had a proposition which might interest the Mormons. After the colony chose their land and surveyed it into lots and sections, they were to keep the even-numbered lots or sections and he and his company (the A. G. Benson Company of New York City) were to be granted the odd-numbered parcels. For this consideration the Postmaster General and his company would give the *Brooklyn* the privilege of leaving New York.

"It's war time, and for American citizens to sail for Mexican territory might be considered the open act that would start a shooting war," he said as he rubbed the palms of his cushiony hands, adding, "It might be my duty as a public servant to also stop Brigham Young and his cohorts from leaving Illinois. Think it over."

"I'll write to President Young. I have no authority to dicker for the whole church," replied Brannan.

"My company will handle all correspondence from our New York office. Good day, Mr. Brannan," said the official as he turned to a file near his desk. Brannan was well aware of the danger they faced.

Brannan, and also the A. G. Benson Company, wrote voluminous letters to Brigham Young, who ignored them both. Brannan confided his fear of Benson to Captain Richardson, who only snickered, filled his nostrils with snuff, and said. "Who does he think he's bluffin'? Not me."

On the stormy morning of February 4th, the captain ran up the flag and gave signals that the *Brooklyn* was weighing anchor. At her stern fluttered the destination pennant of "Oregon." She slipped out of her berth, passed the government offices, and headed out onto the stormy, churning Atlantic. The Mormons sitting around the big table were singing the soul-satisfying hymn, *"How Firm A Foundation, Ye Saints of the Lord."*

> Fear not, I am with thee, O, be not dismayed.
> For I am thy God, and will still give thee aid;
> I'll strengthen thee, help thee, and cause thee to
>   stand,
> Upheld by my righteous, omnipotent hand.

Families gathered to their own cubicles. Laura and Isaac Goodwin gathered their brood of seven small children into their crowded quarters. Colonel Jackson,[1] his wife, and their baby slept on their hard shelf berth for the first time as did all the others, but their spirits were light, and their prayers full of gratitude. Sarah Burr had taken her three-year-old son's hand and walked courageously up the gang plank knowing that another baby was to be born within three weeks and that there was no doctor on the *Brooklyn.* (John) Atlantic Burr was born on the ocean and named for it. When little Atlantic Burr was three weeks old, his three-year-old brother died and was buried at sea.

The Saints were to see many of their dear ones lowered into the cold, unimpressionable ocean. Silas Aldrich died and left small children; Elias Ensign and his grown daughter died, leaving a widow and a young son; and Nancy Narramore's husband died, leaving her alone with a small baby. Most of the deaths were among children. Yet the weary pilgrims met these trials with faith and equanimity. On the occasion of the death of a young man dying at sea a woman wrote a dirge which was long sung among the church people and which was included in some local anthologies:

_____

[1]Women of Mormondom, page 447 by Joyce.

The Dying Californian

(Song of the *Brooklyn* Saints)

Lie up nearer, brother, nearer
For my limbs are growing cold.
And your presence seems the dearer
When your arms around me fold.
I am dying, brother, dying.
Soon you'll miss me in your berth,
And my form will soon be lying
'Neath the ocean's briny surf.

Tell my father when you meet him
That in death I prayed for him
Prayed that I might some day meet him,
In a world that's free from sin.
Tell my mother, God assist her
Now that she is growing old,
Say her child would glad have kissed her
Ere his lips grew pale and cold.

Tell my sister I remember
Every kind and parting word,
And my heart has been kept tender
As my thoughts of memory stirred.
Listen, brother, closely listen
'Tis my wife I speak of now,
Tell her, tell her, how I missed her
When the fever burned my brow.

O my children, God bless them;
They recall my life to me,
O could I but once caress them
Ere I sink below the sea.
Hark! I hear my Savior calling
For his voice I know full well.

When I'm gone then don't be weeping
Brother, here's my last farewell.

After being at sea four months scurvy broke out
among the Mormons and the water supply became low.
Captain Richardson planned to sail straight up the Chilean
Coast to Valparaiso. A hurricane of unusual fierceness
broke without warning. The *Brooklyn* was tossed around
like a peanut shell. Captain and crew despaired of weath-
ering the storm. The captain descended the ladder to prepare his passengers for death. It was at this point that he
found the Mormons singing "God Moves in a Mysterious
Way."

While the ship weathered the storm, the storm brought
tragedy to Laura Goodwin, mother of seven children. She
was thrown down a hatchway while carrying her small
child and was fatally injured. She died the night before
the *Brooklyn* put into the harbor of Mas a Terra, on an
island in the Juan Fernandez Islands, where the hurricane
had blown the *Brooklyn*. It was on this island that Alexander Selkirk, the real Robinson Crusoe, had lived and
awaited his rescue ship.

The island was glorious in its May autumnal foliage.
It had once been a Chilean prison island. Two or three
Chilean families lived there. They welcomed visitors with
their native hospitality and ready sympathy. They, also
the captain and crew of the *Brooklyn*, joined the Mormons
in the funeral service for Laura Goodwin. This was the
first Mormon sermon preached in the Southern Hemisphere. The natives listened with reverent attention; the
seafaring men could not comprehend the Latter-day Saints'
faith in a literal resurrection, but they felt security in the
promise. Grief, like joy, is a universal language—it needs
no interpreter.

To the sea-weary immigrants it was wonderful to feel
the good earth beneath their feet once more—to drink fresh

water and eat newly dug potatoes and vegetables. The few days that the *Brooklyn* lay over in Juan Fernandez Antarctic Indian summer passed quickly. With fond adieus the good ship set sail for the Hawaiian Islands. They crossed the equator for the second time in four months and into the tropical ease and hospitality of the Sandwich islands. The most memorable event on the Pacific was the birth of a baby girl, Pacific (Georgiana) Robbins.

The *Brooklyn* stopped at Honolulu long enough to unload the cargo from New York. Commodore Stockton informed them that the United States and Mexico were at war. He advised them to buy guns and ammunition, and that Brannan organize his men into military companies and drill them. Brannan did this between Honolulu and California until Captain Richardson stopped it.

The cruise from Hawaii was made in six weeks. It was an established travel lane, despite the fact that it had never been mapped. During the three and a half centuries of Spanish rule, they had not surveyed the coastal waters, built a lighthouse, nor planted a beacon or buoy. In that day skippers used old English maps, globes, or school atlases or geographies of which there were few.

The exiles were exuberant with joy when informed that they were near the end of the long, dreary voyage. They gathered around the long table in their quarters and, in reminiscence, relived the six months since they had left New York. Experiences brought laughter or tears—some had suffered sorrows that even the years could not erase. Brannan made fantastic predictions of the fabulous future ahead of them.

Dawn slipped into the world almost unnoticed. Rapidly the sun rose above the fog. The summer-brown peaks of Mount Davidson, Mount Diablo, and Twin Peaks glowed like coral isles in a misty sea. A brisk wind soon dispelled the fog. San Francisco Bay lay placid as a summer pool. The *Brooklyn* glided in smoothly on the incoming tide.

In the meantime there was excitement and conjecture as men scurried into the longboats of the sloop of war, *Portsmouth* (anchored in San Francisco Bay which had been dispatched to intercept the incoming ship. The lookout at the top of Alta Loma (Telegraph Hill) had seen the ship through his spyglass. As the usual summer fog seemed unusually dense this morning, he could not tell whether the ship was friendly or not. Thus he had immediately signaled the *Portsmouth* in the "Cove." Soon the boats sent from the *Portsmouth* reached the *Brooklyn*. An officer climbed up the Jacob's ladder and announced: "May I inform you that you are in the territory of the United States. On July 9, just three weeks ago, Captain John B. Montgomery landed here with seventy sailors and marines and took possession of Yerba Buena in the name of the United States." He was interrupted by cheers from the Mormons and the crew. Many women shed tears and the children shouted. "We hauled down the Mexican flag and ran up our own without firing a shot, or offending a citizen. You are the second ship to come through the gate under the United States flag. The *Olga*, a hide drogher, came a little ahead of you," he concluded.

"Then we're the first colonists under the American regime?" asked Glover.

"You are," replied the officer, "but you are also the first Anglo-Americans to come to California's shores by water."

After military formalities and identification, the officer took Captain Richardson, his aides, and Elder Samuel Brannan and his council to the *Portsmouth* to be interviewed by Captain Montgomery, and the *Brooklyn* was permitted to enter port. Brannan assured Captain Montgomery of the Mormons' loyalty and of their intention to develop the country and be upright citizens. They were willing to do military service and give their lives for their country, if necessary. He told of Commodore Stockton's

advice, which they had followed. He offered to surrender
the arms, ammunition, and the six pound brass cannon
bought in Hawaii. Captain Montgomery ordered all Mormon men enlisted into the armed forces of the United
States, not to serve as regulars, but to serve on night patrol,
if needed. They were to muster at the barracks at a
given signal, armed and equipped for duty.

The Mormons served on only one occasion. Captain
Montgomery had forbidden any man, officer or enlisted,
to bring intoxicating liquor aboard the *Portsmouth*. A
petty officer was in the habit of smuggling a bottle of whiskey aboard when he returned to the ship late at night.
He had a password with a certain bartender. A nonchalant
remark, "The Spaniards are in the brush," meant that the
bartender was to leave a bottle of whiskey under a clump
of wild cherry at the rear of the grog shop. One day, when
the bartender had been busier than usual, he forgot to put
the bottle under the bush. The angry petty officer knocked
on the door to awaken the sleeping bartender, but it
was of no avail. Then he called softly with no results.
Finally, he yelled at the top of his voice with loud profanity,
"The blankety-blank Spaniards are in the brush, you so and
so!" The alert Mormons on night patrol grabbed their
guns. They ran madly into the night without stopping to
dress, spraying the darkness with their bullets. Luckily,
there were no fatalities as San Francisco was sparsely settled at that time.

Captain Montgomery invited the Mormons to visit
the *Portsmouth* the next day (Sunday). There was no
chaplain on the *Portsmouth*, but it was the custom to call
the men on deck and have a printed sermon read. No
work was done in port on the Sabbath. The Mormons
gladly accepted the invitation. The quarter-deck of the
Portsmouth was cleared, a canvas was spread on the deck,
and chairs were brought from the cabins and ward rooms

for the women and children. The men were to sit on capstan bars or on the canvas.

The crew of the *Portsmouth* teased each other about dating a Mormon woman and *growing horns*. To their surprise the women were married, modest, and more interested in their own children. One old gunner growled as he saw them, "Well, tarnation! They don't look 'quair' at all. Just as refined and pretty as women in other churches." Captain Montgomery served lunch to all, and then he took them on a tour of his ship. Lasting friendships were established at the time.

The following Sunday, August the 8th, the Mormons began holding church services in Casa Grande, a large white house that Brannan had rented for his family. This is said to be the first non-Catholic church service held in San Francisco. Religious services were held at the Mission Dolores four miles away. Even after the missions were secularized by the Mexican government, the priests returned to their dilapidated mission for special services. Yet it is quite certain the Mormon service on that August Sabbath was the first non-Catholic service held. From then on Sunday services were held regularly.

The morning after arrival Captain Montgomery sent a large detail of men from the *Portsmouth* to help the Mormons unload the *Brooklyn*. One of the men left a written account: "The cargo of the *Brooklyn* consisted of the most heterogeneous mass of material ever crowded together. In fact it seemed like the ark of Noah. It contained representation of every living thing the mind of man had ever conceived of: agricultural and manufacturing tools in profuse abundance, dry goods, hardware, groceries, candles, seed wheat (soldered up), truck, garden, and grass seed; a printing press, type, paper and all appurtenances, Bibles, school supplies, a library of 179 volumes (the gift of J. M. Van Cott of Philadelphia); sawmill irons, two gristmills, blacksmith tools, carpenter tools, and small stores too nu-

THE FIRST SCHOOL HOUSE.

Erected on the Plaza in 1847.

Built on land donated by Elder Samuel Brannan, carpenter work done by
Elder William Glover, Brannan's first counselor. One hundred children came
on the Mormon chartered ship *Brooklyn* to Yerba Buena, July 31, 1846—
Glover, also William Clark of the *Brooklyn* on San Francisco's first city council.

merous to mention were dug out of the hold and scattered along the beach." (The harrow from the hold of the *Brooklyn* was the first implement of that type ever seen in California, a great curiosity to all who saw it.)

The muscle and strength of almost every man in the hospitable little hamlet of Yerba Buena was required to bring the heavy "Hoe" flat hand printing press to the old mill building and inch it pantingly up to the second floor. (This old press is said to be at the University of Washington, Seattle, Washington, at the present time.) This press was the pride of Brannan's heart. By September Brannan published government bulletins for the military forces. In October he got out an extra (the first in California) announcing his intention to publish a weekly newspaper. This, *The California Star*, was the first newspaper in San Francisco; it began regular publication on January 9, 1847. San Francisco's Hall of Records stands on that site today.

The women made campfires and began cooking for their families. The Mormons had more than doubled the population of Yerba Buena. Fourteen families moved into the abandoned customs house on the Plaza, known as the "Old Adobe." Other families moved from Yerba Buena to the Mission Dolores, four miles away. Here in a dilapidated out-building of the secularized mission Angelina Lovett taught the first school in California where the English language was used. Credit for initiating the first school of this sort usually is given to Mrs. Isobell, who opened such a school at the Santa Clara Mission, fifty miles to the south, some months later. Many families obtained military tents, which they pitched in straight rows. This gave the semblance of a military establishment amongst the crooked trails of Yerba Buena, then called the "Cove" by seafaring men.

Chapter II

In the Wake of the "Brooklyn"

The exuberance of being on land, of being free from prejudice and mob violence, and the bright hopes for a new life brought contentment for a while. However, the glow gradually passed as the Mormons faced the realities of pioneer life and the sudden impact of the fact that they had a large indebtedness to pay. The storms of the Atlantic had delayed them and run the charter costs of the *Brooklyn* into a sum beyond their ability to pay. They owed Captain Richardson a large amount of money. In addition, individual members had little money of their own. While at sea, Brannan had persuaded the people to pool their money into a "company," The S. Brannan Company. This, he had convinced them, was for the good of the group and the protection of all. Financial control, plus the fact that as "first elder" he had religious superintendency, made him almost a dictator.

The Mormons had skilled and willing hands, but there was no employment for them in California. After much "dickering" Captain Richardson agreed to accept a cargo of redwood lumber in payment. Brannan immediately "called" a group of able-bodied men to leave their families in Yerba Buena and go to the sawmill on the Sausalito side of the bay near present day Mill Valley to cut, saw, and load a sufficient amount of redwood to pay Captain Richardson.

Through military circles, the Saints at Yerba Buena learned of the progress of the thousands of Mormons on the prairies, who had left Nauvoo, Illinois, on February 4, 1846, the same day that the *Brooklyn* had sailed from New York. (This had not been arranged—those at Nauvoo started because solid ice bridged the Mississippi River, and the *Brooklyn* had been delayed.)

When war was declared on Mexico on May 13th, President Polk called for 50,000 volunteers. Senator Benton of Missouri, chairman of the Armed Forces Committee, recommended that 1,000 of these volunteers be recruited from the homeless Mormon emigrants then plodding across the Iowa prairies. The "Missouri Mounted" soldiers feared that this proportion was too large. Senator Benton compromised and five companies were requested — a full battalion of 500 men. This was raised, but it weakened the manpower of the Mormon pioneers to the extent that they were forced to establish winter quarters at what would someday be known as Florence, Nebraska, intending to leave for Upper California the following spring.

Brannan was endowed with many qualifications, but, above all, he was an opportunist. He had formed intimate relationships with the U. S. ex-vice consul William Ludesdorff, and also with recently arrived Americans like Melles, Howard, Davis, and others who saw limitless possibilities in Yerba Buena and the matchless harbor of San Francisco Bay. They spoke of it as the "Liverpool of the Pacific," "Gateway to the Orient," and the "New York" or "Philadelphia of the West." These expressions were to last through the years that followed.

Under American regime the Plaza was bounded, and the streets were named Washington, Clay, Kearney, and Montgomery. These were the first four streets in San Francisco. The name of the Plaza was changed to Portsmouth Square in honor of Montgomery's sloop of war.

Brannan's press printed many bulletins and official documents. Most memorable of these was the invitation, or menu (as some called it), for Commodore Sloat's reception, when because of ill-health he turned his command over to Commodore Stockton and prepared to return to the States. It is said that these invitations were printed on

satin with gold lettering by Brannan.   Many women of the
ship *Brooklyn* were guests at that brilliant affair, along
with the vivacious California senoritas who came, some
from faraway haciendas, in their silks, shawls, and jeweled
slippers.

Brannan felt his own importance as leader of the newly deposited colony of Mormons.   He "called" a group of
the brethren to build a house for him on a lot he had purchased adjoining the Plaza. He donated the rear of this lot
as a site for a schoolhouse, which was completed the next
year (1847).   This was the first regular schoolhouse in
California where English was taught.   Angelina Lovett
had, of course, opened her school in an outbuilding of the
Mission Dolores earlier.   Miss Lovett later married Mr.
Kettleman, also a passenger on the *Brooklyn*.

Brannan kept "calling" men to do his bidding.   Many
began to murmur against his ruthless abuse of authority.
Many preferred to work for themselves.   With his inimi-
table oratory he convinced the Mormon congregation of
their responsibility of selecting a site for the *New Zion*,
and of having it in readiness for the delayed 15,000 Saints
detained on the prairies.   He was shrewd enough to fore-
see that a united effort of the group would silence the
tongues of those who questioned his dictatorial procedures.

From those who had explored the great San Joaquin
Valley Brannan learned that it was a vast wonderland, more
than a hundred miles wide, and hundreds of miles long, and
that it extended from the high mountains almost to the
ocean.   Its timber-lipped rivers all emptied into San Francisco Bay, which would give the Mormon *Zion* easy access
to the sea. Mowry and others were ship-conscious men,
but Brannan visualized commercial supremacy of his people on the great river system which drained the valley.
Indians were few, friendly, and they hugged the streams.
Otherwise, the land was vacant and unwanted.

The mission founders had not considered the San

NEW HOPE -1846-
FIRST WHEAT

APPROXIMATELY SIX MILES WEST TWENTY MORMON
PIONEERS FROM SHIP BROOKLYN FOUNDED FIRST KNOWN
AGRICULTURAL COLONY IN SAN JOAQUIN VALLEY. PLANT-
ED FIRST WHEAT. ALSO CROPS THEY IRRIGATED BY POLE
AND BUCKET METHOD. ERECTED THREE LOG HOUSES.
OPERATED SAWMILL AND FERRY ACROSS STANISLAUS.
SETTLEMENT LATER KNOWN AS STANISLAUS CITY.

STATE REGISTERED LANDMARK NO. 436

TABLET PLACED BY CALIFORNIA CENTENNIALS COMMISSION.
BASE FURNISHED BY ALAMEDA COUNTY CAMPS.
DAUGHTERS UTAH PIONEERS
DEDICATED OCTOBER 22. 1949

Joaquin Valley at all in planning their mission system from San Diego to Sonoma. In an interview with Captain John C. Fremont, with whom he had become very friendly, the captain said to Brannan, "Two years ago, on my first trip over the Sierras I camped at the confluence of the San Joaquin and Stanislaus (Rivers). It was scenic as Switzerland, balmy as Italy, and fertile as the Nila Delta."

In the early autumn 1846 Brannan rode into the San Joaquin Valley. At Marsh's Landing (Antioch) Dr. Marsh convinced him of the feasibility of buying a discarded whaleboat, converting it into a sailing launch, and sailing up the San Joaquin. Brannan "called" a crew to convert the whaleboat and to take implements, sawmill irons, seed wheat, and a small flouring mill to "New Hope" on the Stainislaus. (There is a tradition, neither proved, nor disproved, that this little, steel flour mill was sold later at Stockton, and purchased in 1849 by Austin Sperry, owner of a general store and feed yard. Sperry's store and mill burned in 1852. He rebuilt a larger establishment in the same year, which grew into the Sperry Flour Company, now a part of General Mills. All of Sperry's records prior to 1852 are lost. The mill stones of the second mill are now in the walk in front of the Academy of Science in San Francisco, California.)

The sailing launch *Comet* started up the San Joaquin before the autumn rains came. That year was one of early storms as the Donner tragedy proved. The launch started from Marsh's Landing. Brannan had "called" twenty men to go to New Hope to plant wheat, vegetables, and redtop, a forage crop. He set Quartus Sparks "apart" to go to Livermore to buy a yoke of oxen and a span of mules.

Sparks rode one mule and led the other on which another man rode. They had only one bridle. The other man later became Judge Peckham of San Jose. He had deserted ship in San Francisco Bay and was in hiding. Since he was hungry and cold, Sparks had befriended him.

Historic marker to "The Comet" at Mossdale dedicated October 22, 1949.
Plaque reads as follows, "First known sail launch to ascend San Joaquin River
from San Francisco landed here autumn 1846 carried twenty Mormon Pioneers
who founded New Home agricultural project on Stanislaus. Yoke of oxen and
span of mules driven from Marsh's landing (Antioch) by two men who followed
crude map drawn by Merritt the trapper two years later. Doak and Bonsell
operated here the first ferry on San Joaquin River.

"We can't pay wages, but I'm told there's plenty of elk, deer, ducks, geese, doves, and bear up there, and bear lard is whiter than hog's lard any day. You won't starve, and it's the last place on the good green earth that hellish skipper would suspect you of being."

Sparks and Peckham rode around the Bay to Santa Clara Mission. Here Sparks bought Peckham some shoes. From Santa Clara they rode the mission trail to Mission San Jose. Then, while searching for the hacienda of Don Roberto Livermore, they became lost. There were but two white men in the Livermore Valley—Livermore (English) and Amador (Spanish). In the darkness they stumbled onto Amador's home. The gracious Californian invited them to spend the night with him. In the morning he gave them breakfast, and provided them with a guide to accompany them to Don Roberto's. Amador could not talk English, nor could his guests understand Spanish, yet it was an unforgettable occasion for the two travelers.

Sparks and Peckham met Brannan and the others at Marsh's Landing. From Marsh's Landing Sparks and his helper drove the oxen and mules over the trail-less country into the valley. This took two days. After two days on the river the *Comet* stopped at what later became Mossdale, where the trail between Sutter's (Sacramento) and San Jose crossed the river. A state registered landmark on state highway 120 now marks the spot:

"The Comet 1846
First Sail Launch"

First known sail launch to ascend San Joaquin River from San Francisco landed here in autumn of 1846. Carried twenty Mormon Pioneers who founded New Hope agricultural project on the Stanislaus. Yoke of oxen and span of mules driven from Marsh's Landing (Antioch) by two men who followed guide map drawn by Merritt the trapper. Two years later Doak

and Bonsell operated here first ferry on San Joaquin
River.

State Registered Landmark No. 437.
Tablet placed by California Centennial Commission.
Base furnished by Alameda County Camp, Daughters
of Utah Pioneers.
Dedicated October 22, 1949.

From where the *Comet* stopped the men carried the
seed wheat, implements, and machinery to the New Hope
site, a distance of about twenty miles. They planted and
fenced about eighty acres of land, sawed lumber, split
shakes, and built three log houses. Heavy floods caused
much loss and discouragement. The men were homesick
and worried about their families in Yerba Buena. Yet, they
stayed and labored on. Peckham left early in the spring,
but in later years wrote in gratitude of his experience. (See
reference to San Jose Pioneer in Bibliography.)
A registered landmark on National Highway 99 reads:

New Hope 1846
First Wheat

Approximately six miles west, twenty Mormon pioneers from Ship *Brooklyn* founded first known agricultural colony in San Joaquin Valley. Planted first
wheat also crops they irrigated by pole and bucket
method. Erected three log houses, operated sawmill
and ferry across Stanislaus. Named settlement New
Hope. Settlement later known as Stanislaus City.

State Registered Landmark No. 436.
Tablet placed by California Centennial Commission.
Base furnished by Alameda County Camp, Daughters of
Utah Pioneers.
Dedicated October 22, 1949.

Brannan went to the New Hope settlement in April. During the winter he had been brought into court to give an accounting to some church members for his highhanded methods of using church funds. This was the second trial by jury in California. It ended in a hung jury as some of the jurors did not speak English and had to have it translated for them.

The California Star, Brannan's newspaper, was being issued regularly, and a "booster" had been issued and sent to the East. Brannan's big house was completed; many of the malcontents had become tired of being "called" for his projects and started out on their own. Brannan's interest in the growing city of San Francisco took more and more of his time, and he began delegating routine church matters to his counselors and to committees.

After seeing the progress of the colony project at New Hope Brannan decided to ride out on the prairies and conduct Brigham Young to "Zion—New Hope on the Stanislaus." When he struck the bleak Salt Lake Valley, Brannan felt that he would have no trouble convincing President Young, when he compared New Hope with the gray, barren Salt Lake Valley—hedged in my mountains and desicated with a "dead sea" in the center. Brigham Young had seen neither California nor the Salt Lake Valley, but he ignored Brannan's plea and said, "I'll know the place. We will need isolation to grow as we should."

Brannan was angry and felt sure that Brigham Young and his poverty-stricken 15,000 pioneers would be starved into coming to California. Because he knew that President Young mistrusted him, revenge rankled in Brannan's breast as he returned to California. He no longer had faith in the Church, and he was determined to exact retribution from the organization and every member of it. By a strange quirk of fate he did. He pretended to officiate in church affairs for a brief period, but he deceived few of the Mormons. The S. Brannan Company with its agricultural ven-

ture, the *Comet*, the ferry, the tannery interest at San Jose,
farm machinery, grist mills, library, Bibles, and all small
stores were advertised and sold. Many contributors claimed
they got nothing. I never found a statement where any
member was paid. Soon after the fateful January 24, 1848,
when gold was discovered at Coloma, Brannan cut all connections with the Mormons—the church and the people.
However, Brannan's relations with the Mormons immediately following the gold strike will be discussed later.

After Brannan's meeting with Brigham Young he
turned his attention and matchless leadership to money-
making. He opened the first store (as such) in an out-
building of Sutter's Fort (Sacramento) which minted him
money when gold was discovered nearby a few months
later. He speculated in real estate, principally town lots
in San Francisco and Sacramento and the Hawaiian Islands,
when these places mushroomed from tarpaper shacks into
overgrown cities. He, with Osburn, opened-up an im-
porting and merchandising business with China.

In 1851 Brannan visited Honolulu and invested in
extensive real estate and other property in the Hawaiian
Islands. He traveled in Europe and brought sheep, wine
grapes, and many trees and plants to California. These
vines initiated the wine industries in California, especially
that of the famed Napa Valley. He bought 3,000 acres in
Napa Valley, including the famous hot springs near which
he built a mansion house, guest houses, race track, and an
amusement park. He combined the words California and
Saratoga into the name Calistoga for his famous spa. From
Abel Stearns he purchased 160,000 acres of land in Los
Angeles County, California, which he subdivided into
small agricultural tracts. Many elegant buildings were
erected by Brannan in San Francisco and Sacramento. He
even built the noted Capital Hotel (long a landmark in
Sacramento) at a cost of $105,000. Within its elaborate

walls Sacramento held its first grand balls. His love and
faith in California were boundless.

Samuel Brannan was one of the prime movers in organizing the first Vigilance Committee in San Francisco. It
was a lawless method of ending lawlessness which engulfed
California after Fate took life by the bottom of the bag
and shook good, bad, and worse upon its shores during the
gold rush. He was interested in all political and civic adventures. He gave money, and was a director of the Academy of Science; he helped organize and became president
of the California Society of Pioneers; he printed San Francisco's first newspaper; sponsored its first book of verse,
Poetry of the Pacific (after a limited little volume, "Out-
croppings"); he built the first Cliff House in 1854; and he
was connected with numerous other literary, cultural, and
educational beginnings. He even bought fire-fighting
equipment and was a volunteer fireman. He was quick in
sympathy and free with money—an easy touch for all.

In 1853 Brannan was elected state senator; he was a
Lincoln elector in Lincoln's second election. He went from
rags to riches to rags during his forty-three years in California. He was once considered the richest man in the
state. He gave generously to all civic and cultural enterprises attempted or dreamed of. He was always willing
to help the down and out. Many whom he had befriended
shunned him when his pockets were empty and their own
were filled. He kept his pride and spirit of romance, however. When old and penniless, he came to San Francisco
to borrow money from relatives. In braggadocio he told
a reporter that he had obtained a large amount of money
due him from the Mexican government and was in "the city"
squaring old accounts. This story was played up by the
press, and has been accepted as history.

Soon afterwards, Brannan returned to San Diego an
ill and broken man (see story *Samual Brannan and the
Golden Fleece*). He died in 1889. For lack of money to

bury him his remains lay unclaimed for a year. His nephew, Alexander Badlam, eventually gave him a Christian burial.[1] In 1926 a marker was placed at his grave in Mount Hope Cemetery, San Diego, California. It reads: "Sam Brannan 1819-1889, California Pioneer of 1846. Dreamer—Leader and Empire-builder."

Brannan's ruthless "calling" of men for worthy projects often imposed untold hardship and grief on the women and children of those men. They were poorly sheltered and often inadequately fed. They were temporarily squatting in a strange land. Many young wives gave birth to children in tents or in crowded quarters of friends. In those days California had no threshing machines. Grain was thrown on the ground, and fast horses raced over it. It was then tossed in the wind to get rid of the chaff. This often left pebbles and particles of horse manure in it. Women carefully picked it over before boiling it to eat. Boiled wheat and molasses was a staple diet to these Mormon pioneers.

Like others, the Mormon women went to the hides piled on the beach waiting for the "Boston Ship" to take them to the Atlantic Coast to be tanned into leather. They cut fat from the cured hides. Colonel Jackson's wife wrote, "I soaked mouldy ship bread I had purchased from a whaling ship in the Bay and fried it in tallow taken from the rawhides lying on the beach. God made it sweet to me and to

---

[1] I quote from a San Francisco paper (*Chronicle*). "In 1956 Superior Judge Albert C. Wollenberg of San Francisco approved the appointment of Frank Rerstrom as one of the five trustees of a grant made to the Independent Order of Odd Fellows in 1860 by Sam Brannan, San Francisco pioneer—at 1019 and 1023 Mission Street, between Sixth and Seventh Streets, San Francisco. In 1860 it was valued at $200.00, today it is worth $500,000 and brings an income of about $600.00 per month.—Under trust the I.O.O.F. can never sell the property—Brannan died broke. . . . He is often credited with being San Francisco's first millionaire. He came to San Francisco as leader of 238 Mormons. The town was then Yerba Buena. This was three weeks after it had become American territory and had a population of only 60 Americans. He gave San Francisco its first newspaper. . . . From newspaper publishing he went into business of high finance; he helped finance the Juarez movement against Napoleon III."

Yet he died alone, so to speak. No fraternal order or friend came forth with money in his illness and old age.

my child, for on this food I weaned her. It made me think of Hagar and her babe and of the God who watched over her." (*Heart Throbs,* Vol. III, p. 203.)

The colonel's wife adds: "During the winter of 1846, I lived in a house near the Plaza." Here Dr. Powell (for whom Powell Street, San Francisco, is named) had a sanitarium where he brought seriously ill naval personnel. Dr. Powell was attached to the sloop of war *Warren,* but was allowed to live ashore. This establishment of Dr. Powell's was undoubtedly the first hospital in Yerba Buena. Mrs. Jackson tells also of her first Christmas dinner in California. A hospital steward of Dr. Powell's hospital room (in the same house) brought her a quart of beans and a pound of salt pork. He warned her to keep it a secret as he might get flogged for giving away government property. The genial naval surgeon, himself, brought a slice of ham, a drawing of tea, a lump of butter the size of a walnut, and informed them where they could buy a half barrel of flour.

After Mrs. Jackson obtained the flour she mixed up a cake and baked it in the ashes of a campfire between two tin plates. The improvised baking proved successful, so she invited her friend Mrs. Robbins to come and join in the repast. "This is lovely, isn't it? Just like Boston," complimented Mrs. Robbins.

Many Mormons initiated the American way of life in California. John R. Robbins bought land south of Market Street, and owned the site of the present Sheraton-Palace Hotel. It was a mud-hole then. Together with his brothers Charles and Isaac, he bought a horse from an Australian ship for $1,000. With this horse and a cart they started the first express business in San Francisco. It paid them very well, and they were able to take a trip to New Jersey, their home state. Charles R. Robbins remained in San Francisco and worked on the *California Star* as a printer.

John Burr (father of Atlantic Burr) built one of the first permanent homes in Yerba Buena. William Evans

bought land at a place which later became Market and Van
Ness, and opened the first tailor shop. William S. Clark
built a wharf from the waterfront out to what later became
Broadway and Battery Streets, where the ships stopped in
deep water. Jacob Leese had a small stoop at the waterfront at high tide. Clark's Long Wharf was extended from
Leese's stoop, and was long known as Clark's Point.

All sewing was done by hand and most of the women
were seamstresses. Many of them found employment in
this field. Clothing, bedding, drapes, and household linens
were either made or hemmed by hand. The opening of
hotels, rooming houses, etc., drew on these capable women
for time and talents. The contribution of the *Brooklyn*
immigrants to the rescue of the Donner Party, the first
farms, and other events inked into history will be discussed
more fully in subsequent chapters.

The good ship *Brooklyn* passed out of the lives of its
passengers after the indebtedness was paid. Few had reason to remember the long, dreary trip with pleasure. Those
who had slipped the dead bodies of loved ones into the
cold ocean bore unhealable scars in their hearts. The fury
of the raging tempest, the mountainous waves, and the deep
troughs were stamped indelibly on the memories of all.

Few left written accounts as to the fate of the ship
where they had spent six months between decks. Some say
she took her lumber and sailed for "the islands." Others
contend she was unseaworthy and never left the bay. During the gold rush of '49, it is certain that San Francisco
became a morgue and a cemetery for ships. When Bayard
Taylor, world traveler, visited California in 1849, he wrote:
"San Francisco is a forest of spars and deserted ships."

Thomas Eager, seventeen or eighteen years of age
when on the *Brooklyn*, must have retained some pleasant
memories of his trip to California. Some years later, as a
successful businessman and member of the Alameda County Board of Supervisors, he used his influence to perpetuate

Home of Hon. Thomas Eager in Brooklyn (East Oakland)—had town named for the ship which brought him to California, 1846.

the ship's name upon the map of California. I quote from Thompson and West's *Atlas* of Alameda County (California, 1878):

"In 1856 the Board of Supervisors of Alameda County passed a resolution that the town of Clinton and a place called San Antonio be consolidated and the territory embraced by them called *Brooklyn*. Mr. Thomas Eager, a member of the Board, introduced the resolution. He was a passenger on the *Brooklyn,* a ship which in 1846 brought some of our earliest and most respected citizens. It is probable that Mr. Eager designed in this manner to perpetuate the memory of the good ship. . . . With the exception of Washington Township, Brooklyn received the first American as well as the first Spanish . . . permanent settlers west of Alameda Creek."

John M. Horner, also a passenger on the *Brooklyn,* was the first white American to settle in Alameda County. He came with his bride in 1847 and was first in many of his projects. He started many towns in the southern part of the country. In Union, a town he built, he named the first hotel "The Brooklyn House."

It is known that a United States Post Office was established at Brooklyn very early. In the 1850's the mining camp of Red Dog had grown into a town large enough to ask for a post office. The citizens (many from New York) decided on a more dignified name than Red Dog, so they petitioned for the post office in the name of Brooklyn. They were informed that there was already a town of that name.

Thomas Eager entered the lumber business in Santa Cruz, California. The mills in Redwood Canyon* became active as the gold fever burned itself out. Eager came to what is now East Oakland in 1852, and went into the lumber business there near his source of supply. In 1853

----

*The Oakland-Berkeley, Walnut Creek, Hayward two million dollar Tri-Stake Tabernacle dedicated Sept. 25, 1960, is located in what was Brooklyn Township and not far from Redwood Park. The redwood industry was developed as the gold fever subsided.

Thompson, Strode, Jones, Lemoore, and others bought 6,300 acres bounded by Lake Merritt and the estuary in what is now East Oakland. They laid out the townsite of Clinton, extending from the slough to what is now Seventh Avenue. In 1854 he married Angelina Ann Tupper. History records that the home he built for his bride was the first home on the Contra Costa side of the Bay "built with a bay window." It was located at what is now Seventh Avenue and East 12th Street. Later Mr. Eager bought the home of his father-in-law, Harry Tupper, at East 12th Street and 13th Avenue, said to be the first house built between Clinton and San Antonio.

In 1853, when Alameda County was amputated from the original countries of Santa Clara and Contra Costa, Thomas Eager was elected to the Board of Supervisors. Later, he was elected to the California legislature, and served as sergeant-at-arms in the Assembly for some time. His home address is listed as Brooklyn.

Brooklyn increased its size in 1870 by taking the principality of Lynn into its folds. At this time Brooklyn became an incorporated city. It is the parent town from which the great city of Oakland grew. Brooklyn boasted of its schools, homes, industries, and its commercial and recreational advantages. For a brief period of time it was the county seat, during the twenty year battle for the county seat between Brooklyn, New Haven (Alvarado, Union), and Oakland (1853 to 1873). This fight was often settled by the state legislature, rather than by the residents of the county. However, Brooklyn was finally annexed to Oakland by a vote of the people. It was known as Oakland's seventh ward, and also as Brooklyn Township, and extended from the east shore of Lake Merritt to San Leandro, approximately, and along present Park Avenue to near the tunnel, and thence along the country line.

Chapter III

The Mormon Battalion

Within twenty-four hours after the *Brooklyn* dropped anchor in Yerba Buena Cove July 31, 1846 another body of Mormons, the Mormon Battalion, began their march of 2,100 miles from Fort Leavenworth, August 1846, (in the frontier country which later became Kansas) to San Diego, California. This was, perhaps, one of the longest infantry marches in history.

"Bonaparte crossed the Alps, but these men have crossed a continent," with these words Colonel Philip St. George Cook presented the Mormon Battalion to General Stephen W. Kearney, when the General reviewed the troops in Los Angeles in May, 1847. Colonel Cook had commanded the Mormon Battalion from Santa Fe to the Pacific Coast. Their assignment had been the building of a wagon road from the edge of civilization to California for the purpose of transporting supplies to the army stationed in California, during the war with Mexico. This vacant, trackless waste was marked on the map as the "Great American Desert."

The Mormon Battalion had been recruited from the camp of an exiled Mormon emigrant train wending its way to a "New Zion" they expected to establish somewhere "beyond the outmost bounds of the everlasting hills." None had ever seen the "New Zion," but they knew it would be in *The Upper California*, then a territory of Mexico. They had been dispossessed, were underfed, poorly clad, and, because of constant mobbing and privation, the exiles were short of manpower to combat life in the hostile wilderness. To furnish their quota of one per cent (500 men) of the 50,000 volunteers requested by the government meant the loss of teamsters, wagoners, and trail-breakers. It took fathers, husbands, and young sons from aged and incapacitated parents. It meant the loss of providers and protectors of children and wives in a hostile, unexplored environment. Yet the full quota was raised in a week's time. The sacrificing of 500 "young able bodied men," weakened the traveling power of the emigrants to the extent that they were forced to establish winter quarters near Council Bluffs, Iowa. This delayed their journey to the Salt Lake Valley by one year.

On July 11, 1846, Colonel Thomas L. Kane, who had been sent from Washington, D. C. to General Kearney at Fort Leavenworth, reached Council Bluffs. With him was Captain Allen with whom General Kearney had sent "a circular to the Mormons." The Battalion was mustered in, and Captain Allen took the organization under his command on July 16, 1846. Undoubtedly Senator Benton of Missouri, head of the powerful Armed Forces Committee (there was no chief of staff in those days) used his office to avenge his smoldering grudge against his old enemy— the Mormons.

The United States declared war on Mexico on May 13, 1846, after Mexico's attack on General Zachary Taylor at Resaca de la Palma and Palo Alto on the 8th and 9th of May. This was considered an act of hostility against the United States which had not been at war, but had merely been patrolling the frontier. The army was small and not up to war strength. It was necessary for President Polk to call for 50,000 volunteers with an allotment to each state. It has been said that Senator Benton first requested that 1,000 men be called from the Mormon emigrants on the prairies. The Missouri mounted troops feared that, if the Mormons were too large in number, they might retaliate for the persecution that the Mormons had suffered in Missouri. Thus General Kearney was instructed to enlist volunteers from the exiled Mormons only to the extent of one third of his force.

Colonel Thomas L. Kane was ordered to proceed to Fort Leavenworth with the orders for Kearney. He reached St. Louis, Missouri, the 26th of June and rode on to the "Fort." From there he rode to the Mormon camp on the Iowa prairies. Captain Allen accompanied him to enroll the battalion and take command of it. Brigham Young, the Mormon leader, welcomed the opportunity to prove the loyalty of the Mormon people, regardless of the persecutions which certain states had perpetrated on them. The flag of the United States was produced from its hiding place in a covered wagon, hung from a tree, and the volunteers were enlisted beneath its enfolding ripples. There were tears, cheers, and speeches. Brigham Young said, "Let it be distinctly understood that the organization of the Mormon Battalion will prove our loyalty to the United States—Let the Mormons be the first to set foot in California. . . ."

The battalion was to be part of the regular army with its pay of $7.00 per month (a little less than 25 cents per day), $3.50 per month clothing allowance, or $42.00 per year, was allowed each man also. The full quota of men was filled. On July 20th the 500 men left for Fort Leavenworth as the sun set in a blaze of glory where the earth and sky met on the limitless plains. On July 31st, or thereabouts (personal journals vary from the 31st of July to August 1st), they began the long march to the Pacific Coast. The battalion drew its full year of clothing allowance and sent it back to their destitute families at Council Bluffs, and began their march in the tattered clothes and worn shoes in which they had left Nauvoo, Illinois. The sharp rocks and cacti of the desert soon wore out the shoes, and the men made shoes from rawhide, animal skins, or discarded canvas. They rejoiced that they had been able to send more than two thousand dollars to their destitute loved ones.

The paymaster at Fort Leavenworth was amazed to see that each man could sign his own name on the pay roll, an unusual thing in those days. Each of the battalion men carried his blankets, a knapsack, a cartridge belt containing many rounds of ammunition, a short ration, and his musket on his back. He opened up a road as he went. In Tyler's journal is recorded: "The deep sand alone without the load was enough to wear out both man and beast. . . . At times we had twenty men with long ropes to each wagon (supply wagons) to help the teams pull the wagons over the sand hill." One of the battalion celebrates the incidents in doggerel verse:

> "Our hardships reach their rough extremes,
> When valiant men are roped with teams,
> Hour after hour day by day,
> To wear our strength and lives away.

> "We see some twenty men or more
> With empty stomachs and footsore
> Bound to one wagon plodding on
> Through sand beneath the burning sun."

The death of Captain Allen on August 23rd was a real tragedy to the battalion as his successor, Lieutenant Smith, as well as Dr. George, was prejudiced and cruel, and the men suffered in both health and morale. They were foot-sore and at times suffered agonizing thirst. The thirst was often occasioned by regular doses of calomel and arsenic which salivated them and desiccated their bodies in the excessive heat. Yet they were forced to walk on over rocks, sand, and, in the late summer, the alkali dust.

At Santa Fe Colonel Cook took command. Part of the march led through a terrain where man had never been; it ranged from high, timberless, waterless mountains to land below sea level. Cook wrote of it as the "most trying of the march for both man and beast, heavy sands, hot days, cold nights, and short rations." In the narrow passes men used crowbars and pickaxes to widen chasms of living rock narrower than the wagons, and, in addition, helped the exhausted mules pull the wagons. To Cook orders were orders and he permitted no exception—he forced the men on. Passages were cut, according to orders, only to find that they had to be widened, or they were completed only to discover higher mountains and narrower passes ahead with more loose rock to be cleared before a solid footing could be reached. Much equipment and road tools were worn out. They struggled on over mountain, canyon, and desert.

On January 24th they sighted the blue Pacific from a hill above San Luis Rey Mission. The weather, bland and balmy as a May morning, filled their hearts with joy and the satisfaction of accomplishment. They reached San Diego on January 29th, six months after leaving Fort Leavenworth. Colonel Cook issued the following bulletin:

BULLETIN

Headquarters Mormon Battalion
Mission of San Diego
January 30, 1847

(Orders No. 1)

"The Lieutenant-Colonel, commanding, congratulates the Battalion on their safe arrival on the shore of the Pacific Ocean, and the conclusion of their march of over two thousand miles.

"History may be searched in vain for an equal march of infantry. Half of it has been through a wilderness, where nothing but savages and wild beasts are found, or deserts where, for want of water, there is no living creature. There, with almost hopeless labor, we have dug deep wells,

which the future traveler will enjoy. Without a guide who
had traversed them we have ventured into trackless table-
lands where water was not found for several marches. With
crowbar and pick, and axe in hand, we worked our way
over mountains, which seemed to defy aught save the wild
goat, and hewed a pass through a chasm of living rock
more narrow than our wagons. To bring these first wagons
to the Pacific, we have preserved the strength of our mules
by herding them over large tracts, which you have labor-
iously guarded without loss. The garrison of four presidios
of Sonora concentrated within the walls of Tucson, gave
us no pause. We drove them out, with their artillery, but
our intercourse with the citizens was unmasked by a single
act of injustice. Thus, marching half-naked and half-fed,
and living upon wild animals, we have discovered and made
a road of great value to our country.

"Arriving at the first settlements of California, after a
single day's rest, you cheerfully turned off from the route
to this point of promised repose, to enter upon a campaign,
and meet, as we supposed, the approach of an enemy; and
this, too, without even salt to season your sole subsistence
of fresh meat.

"Lieutenants A. J. Smith and George Stoneman, of the
First Dragoons, have shared and given invaluable aid in
all these labors.

"Thus, volunteers, you have exhibited some high and
essential qualities of veterans. But much remains undone.
Soon, you will turn your attention to the drill, to system
and order, to forms also, which are all necessary to the
soldier.

"By order
/Signed   "Lieut.-Colonel P. St. George Cook,
/Signed   "P. C. Merrill, Adjutant"[1]
Colonel Cook was a strict disciplinarian, despotic in
command, adamant in his demand for obedience, yet, para-

------

[1]B. H. Roberts, *The Mormon Battalion*, The Deseret News, Salt Lake
City, Utah, 1919, pp. 52-53.

doxically, he was kindhearted and loved his men. This was proved ten years later (1857), when a misinformed president sent an army into Salt Lake to "subdue" what he thought was a rebellion among the Mormons. When Johnston's Army rode through Salt Lake City on that fateful day in 1857, Colonel Philip St. George Cook removed his hat and rode bareheaded out of respect to the Mormon Battalion which he had commanded ten years before.

After being discharged the battalion men rapidly traveled towards where they thought their co-religionists would settle—the Salt Lake Valley. Many came north to where some of the Mormons had settled the year before. The journal of John Barrowman is typical of those who came to San Francisco in the late summer of 1847. He tells of attending services of the Latter-day Saint Church in San Francisco and of business and social contacts with the Kettlemans, Sirrine, Clark, and Austin. He also told of working for William Glover and later for the Mowry brothers who had a launch at Marsh's Landing. Some men recorded incidents of having new "garments" made by the women and of attending meetings where reorganization of the church took place and of how Brannan lectured to the people in regards to their discontent with his leadership. Also, members of the Mormon Battalion found all commodities very expensive in California.

First Sergeant Nathaniel V. Jones of Company D was chosen, among others, to accompany General Kearney "to the states." When Captain John C. Fremont demanded that a controversy between Kearney and Fremont be tried in Washington, D. C., Jones rode back with the party as far as Fort Leavenworth. He kept a day-to-day journal of his round trip from Leavenworth to California and back. He was anxious to return to his wife and children at Council Bluffs, Iowa.

Kearney and Fremont each had his own escort and traveled a short distance apart. They left Los Angeles in

May 1847. Jones vividly describes the drought and heat of the "Great Valley." On July 9th Jones wrote: "This morning we came to the Stanislaus River. I learned there is a settlement of our (Mormon) people about six miles below where we crossed. . . . Came about twenty miles and found some American . . . June 12. Heard that Brother Brannan has gone to pilot the church out here, through the mountains. . . . This evening there was a brother who came to see us by the name of Rhoads. He came here last October from Missouri. The brethren are settled in different places through this (Central California) country.

"On June 17th Kearney's group left Johnson's Ranch (near present Marysville)—at the foot of the mountains there is not another settlement now until we reach Fort Hall (Idaho)." On June 21st they came to the Pass and to the site of the ghastly tragedy of the Donners. The revolting sight that they found there will be discussed later.

Much has been written of the benefits, sacrifices, and suffering of the Mormon Battalion. It is the purpose in this chapter to deal mainly with what happened in California. When their year of enlistment was completed and they were discharged at Los Angeles, they were asked to re-enlist. One company did; the others made immediate plans to join their families, wherever they were. They preferred to try the northern route.

Shortly after Brannan turned his face toward California after his ill-fated meeting with Brigham Young, Captain James Brown, of the detachment of the Mormon Battalion which had wintered at Pueblo, joined Brigham Young on the trail. President Young suspected Brannan, and sent Captain Brown to California to collect money for the families of the Mormon Battalion. He also requested the men to stay in California and get work, if they could, as the Salt Lake Valley was barren and food unobtainable that first winter. Thus, those of the Mormon Battalion who were heading East turned back to look for work in California.

Many men of the battalion found work with Captain Sutter at his fort in New Helvetia (now Sacramento). Sutter had fifty or more ex-battalion men working for him the winter of 1847-48. Many continued to keep up their journals as Brigham Young had advised when they marched away on their long trek. Henry Bigler's journal had far-reaching consequences on world events and legislative decisions years afterward.

Henry Bigler kept his journal from day to day. He wrote on September 27, 1847: "A man came to our quarters and said, 'Captain Sutter wants four men to go into the mountains to build a sawmill on the South Fork of the American River.'"

This was James Marshall, the contractor. He had already sent some of the Mormon Battalion and some Indians ahead. Others were to stop about twenty-five miles from the Fort and build a grist mill. There were, besides Marshall, a dozen white men: Peter Wimmer, the gang boss; Charles Bennett; William Scott; and nine battalion men. Bigler, and others, list the Mormons as Alexander Stephens, James S. Brown, James Barger, William Johnson, Azariah Smith, and Henry Bigler at the sawmill. There may have been others. Bancroft lists Sidney Willis and possibly his brother, Wilford Hudson, and Levi Fifield at the grist mill.

Marshall and Bennett had come to Oregon in 1844. Wimmer and his wife, Elizabeth Jane Wimmer, had come to California in late October 1846 in the Harlan-Fowles emigrant train. Mrs. Wimmer was to cook for the men. Earlier she had lived at the gold mines in Georgia. The men were dissatisfied with her cooking. She explained that the heavy sediment in the water pitcher was not dirt, but quite possibly there was gold in the streams nearby. The men hooted and ridiculed her. Marshall, a rough frontiersman, laughed loudest of all.

On the morning of January 24th, after the water had been run through the flume, Marshall, Wimmer, and the "Battalion Boys" went out to the tailrace to see how successful the venture had proved. As they walked along Peter Wimmer picked up some bright particles. He rolled his eyes and said, "Say, these are heavy! Mebbe it's gold!" The others picked up some and talked about them, handing some to Marshall for his opinion. Mrs. Wimmer's son by a former marriage, John, was tagging along.

"Here, Johnny," said Wimmer, as he handed the largest ones to the boy, "you take them pretty pebbles to your Ma, she'll know whether it's gold or not." Mrs. Wimmer was making soap in an old kettle outside the cook shack.

"I can soon prove it," she said as she tossed the nuggets into the lye and boiling fat. These chemicals proved it was gold. Marshall, an aggressive man of loose habits, ordered everyone to keep silent about the discovery. He gathered the specimens from the men and headed for the Fort to have Sutter test them with acid.

Henry Bigler wrote in his journal: "Monday, January 24. This day some kind of mettle (metal) that looks like gold was found in the tailrace." He also wrote a code letter to his battalion brothers at the grist mill.

Willis, Hudson, and Fifield immediately came up to the sawmill at Coloma. They found a little gold and then returned to their work. On the way back one remarked, "If there is gold up there, it's just as apt to be here." They panned with their tin plates and found gold. This second strike was soon called *Mormon Island.*

Samuel Brannan, the ex-Mormon leader, was an opportunist. He seized upon this find to organize the brethren into an exclusive group, and took over the project at Mormon Island. Many did not know of his apostasy and trusted him as a bona fide church officer. He collected

GOLD DISCOVERY SITE

· STATE HISTORICAL MONUMENT ·

ON JANUARY 24, 1848, GOLD WAS DISCOVERED IN THE TAIL-RACE OF SUTTERS SAWMILL BY JAMES W. MARSHALL. THIS DISCOVERY PRECIPITATED THE FAMOUS GOLD RUSH AND THE INFLUX OF "FORTY-NINERS" INTO CALIFORNIA. SUTTER'S MILL STOOD ON THE RIVER BANK ABOUT 500 FEET NORTHEAST OF THIS POINT. THE SITE MAY BE REACHED BY ANY OF THE MARKED TRAILS WHICH START FROM THIS PARKING AREA.

FOR HISTORICAL EXHIBITS AND FURTHER INFORMATION VISIT THE MUSEUM, ACROSS THE HIGHWAY.

JAMES W. MARSHALL IS BURIED AT THE MARSHALL MONUMENT WHICH STANDS ON THE HILL TO THE SOUTHWEST AND IS VISIBLE FROM THIS POINT. IT IS ALSO IN THE STATE PARK SYSTEM. IT MAY BE REACHED BY ROAD LEAVING THE HIGHWAY SOUTHEAST OF COLOMA.

California State Park Commission

Nine of twelve white men at Coloma when gold was discovered were ex-Mormon Battalion men. Henry Bigler was the only one who recorded the event—"On the spot where it was found." Bigler Journal–Bancroft Library, University of California Berkeley

Mormon Island 1851—second gold strike—now inundated by Folsom Dam—reproduced through the courtesy of the Bancroft Library, University of California, Berkeley, California.

their tithing of ten per cent and talked of contributing more money for church buildings. He laid a foundation for his first million dollars.

All went smoothly for Brannan until the following August (1848), when Governor Mason and his aid William T. ("War Is Hell") Sherman came to Coloma and Mormon Island to get samples of gold to prove that there was wealth in California. Up to that time gold had not been discovered elsewhere in California except for the famous green onion legend in Southern California. There was a furor going on in Congress to have the treaty of Guadalupe-Hidalgo (January 1848), which had ceded Upper California to the United States, abrogated. Many legislators contended that much of the territory was worthless; they insisted also that it was too far from Washington to be governed by "the States" and would be a heavy burden to the taxpayers.

Specimens of gold were gathered at Coloma and Mormon Island. Tradition says that Governor Mason held samples in his hand and asked Elder William Glover to select the most convincing nuggets. The gold nuggets were then soldered into an old tea caddy and given to a sergeant to deliver in Washington, D.C. The sergeant rode to a seaport, took passage on a ship headed for Peru, then re-embarked for Panama, walked over the isthmus, and finally caught a boat for New Orleans. From there he staged to Washington, D. C. with the gold. He delivered it to President Polk on December the first, 1848. The President mentioned the discovery of gold in his "State of the Nation" speech on December 5th. Immediately all ships changed their courses and sailed for California, and all wagons rolled west. The gold rush was on.

After the trusted sergeant rode into the sunset that hot August afternoon, the men at Mormon Island gathered around Governor Mason and General Sherman. "Say, Governor, what right has Sam Brannan to collect tithes from us? How long can he do it?" asked one.

"As long as you Mormons are damned fools enough to pay it," replied the Governor.

"Well, I'll pay no more," said one.

"Me, neither," chorused the crowd. Brannan's deceitful trickery was ended. "His velvet paws now showed his claws." His connection with the Mormon Church and Mormon people was completely severed. He had trampled every tenet and principle of the Church teaching. No church member ever associated with him again, either socially or in business.

Elizabeth Jane Wimmer was never honored for testing the gold in her soap kettle. She kept the largest nugget that went through the soap kettle test. For years she wore it on a chain around her neck, tied in a little buckskin bag. A relative of hers, who wrote a book on the Fowler Mallett family, says, "that on one occasion Mrs. Wimmer refused $2,000 for the nugget, although it was not worth more than about $16.00."

Later, Mrs. Wimmer loaned the nugget to a newspaperman who promised to write the true story of her connection with the discovery of gold at Coloma. The nugget was stolen from him, and lost forever. A replica of it was on display in a case of the California Society of Pioneers for years, but was destroyed by the fire of 1906. Hal Johnson (*Berkeley Daily Gazette,* December 1, 1953) wrote that Mrs. Bessie Hargrave Dury of Walnut Creek, California, also had a replica of the nugget.

The old house where the Wimmers lived in Coloma stood unnoticed and fell into decay, and Mrs. Wimmer's soap kettle rusted away. But, on a hill nearby, the state of California erected a monument to the contractor, Marshall, giving him full credit. He was also given a pension for the rest of his life, notwithstanding that Peter Wimmer and many of the Mormon workmen handed him the specimens he took to Sutter for testing. Mallett comments bitterly that the state of California "subsidized the liquor industry by pensioning Marshall." History has credited Marshall and there it stands. There was no doubt that the discovery of gold changed the course of human events as it brought to California's shores masses of people of every stratum of society and every nation, race, and hybrid on the earth's swirling ball.

In less than two years enough people were in California to warrant statehood without going through the adolescent period of *territorialhood*—a distinction no other state can claim. California had matured to the extent that it was now alert to the value of its landmarks and traditions and to their perpetuation and evaluation. As gold had given birth to the state, the state and such organizations as the Native Sons and Native Daughters of the Golden West began to work for a monument to the discoverer of gold. A monument was dedicated to James W. Marshall on May 3, 1890, at Coloma. Many were dissatisfied with the date carved on the monument. Marshall had said it was "along somewhere between the 18th and 20th of January in '48." Bancroft, and others, thought it later. However, January 19th was carved on the monument. That did not settle the controversy; the wrangle continued.

In 1887 (two years after the senile, old Marshall died) the diary of Henry Bigler came to light. He had noted the discovery of gold, the place of discovery, and the exact day it happened. His diary, previously quoted in this book, placed the date of discovery as the 24th. However, there is another entry for Sunday, January 30, which elaborates upon the find: ". . . our metal has been tried and proven to be gold. It is thought to be quite rich. We picked up more than a hundred dollars last week." The information in Bigler's diary agreed with a notation made by Captain Sutter —that gold was discovered on January 24th. Historians were satisfied. The "19th" was chiseled from the inscription and the "24th" inserted. It looked patchy and agitation began for a new plaque. Finally, the legislature ordered a

new bronze plaque.   In 1939 the new tablet was placed.
It reads:

Erected by the State of California
In Memory of
James W. Marshall
1810-1885
Whose Discovery of Gold January 24, 1848
In The Tailrace of Sutter's Mill at Coloma
Started the Great Rush of Argonauts
Monument Unveiled May 3, 1890

While many Mormons flocked to Mormon Island, they
later prospected in other places.   Their names dotted the
early map of California; there was Mormon Bar in Mariposa County, Mormon Gulch and Mormon Road in Tuol-
umne County, Mormon "Diggins" in Sacramento County
and Mormon Channel (Stockton) in San Joaquin County.
Other places they named, or that were named after them,
are: Mormon Corral, El Dorado County; Desolation Valley (tradition); Mormon Station, Genoa, Nevada; Mormon
Springs, San Bernardino County; Mormon Well, San Diego
County; New Hope, San Joaquin County; Hope Valley,
Pleasant Valley, El Dorado County; Tragedy Springs; and
Mount Joseph Smith, once the name of Mount Palomar.*

The Mormon men under contract to Captain Sutter
often panned for gold on their after hours, but they remained true to their word until they had completed their
contract.   This is evidenced by a legend on the door at
Sutter's Fort today. (Sutter's Fort was restored and is California's Pioneer Museum.)   It reads:

"In 1847-8 the room originally on this location was
used by the Mormons who were working for Captain Sut-

---

*Colorful California Names:
American Trust Co., 1955, "Banking since 1854."
"Palomar–Mountain, location of giant 200 inch Hale telescope–Home of
band tailed pigeons (Pigeon roost) Originally the Mountain was called Smith
Mountain for Joseph Smith, Mormon Leader," page 27.

ter—some of the same Mormons who accompanied James W. Marshall to Coloma to build a sawmill on the American River, in the mill-race upon which was later discovered gold in January 1848.

"Sam Brannan, a Mormon leader in California, had a trading post in a large adobe building outside the Fort grounds. He was one of the most progressive and alert men of his time, and to him much credit is due for . . . his accomplishment in the up-building of this state in the early days.

"Of his Mormon workmen Captain Sutter always spoke very highly. They were industrious, sober, and when the gold strike came and everybody was stampeding to the gold diggings, these Mormons held to their contract with Sutter until their job was done."

The fraternity of the Mormon Battalion lasted long as this newspaper notice reveals:

Notice in *Deseret News,* Salt Lake City, Jan. 25, 1855:

NOTICE TO MORMON BATTALION

"On Tuesday Jan. 10, 1855 several members of the Mormon Battalion convened in the upper room of John M. Horner and Co's store of the Tithing Office Building, to devise ways and means to give a ball and supper to the members of the Battalion . . . under sanction of Governer Brigham Young."

The discovery of gold in California did not change the plans of the Mormon Battalion and some *Brooklyn* Saints to go to the recently established settlement of the Mormons in the Salt Lake Valley. Many had remained in California, because of the counsel of Brigham Young. Some had families languishing back in Winter Quarters, Nebraska, that they had left almost two years before. They gathered gold and impatiently waited for winter to lift her fettering white mantle of snow from the Sierras. They were anxious to begin building homes again. Unlike the Argonauts, who followed them, the Mormons did not plan to scoop-up gold and return to their homes where they had left off. These religious exiles had to begin all over again in a strange and hostile land.

After his discharge from the army in July 1847, Captain Jefferson Hunt rode to the Salt Lake Valley. The vanguard of the Church had arrived there July 24, 1847. After going through Cajon Pass he picked up the old Santa Fe Trail. He then explored a direct route to Salt Lake. It was well-chosen, and most of it became what was later called the "Southern Route." It was used by those who feared the Donner Pass. Hunt had come up to "Sutter's" and mined gold. He became the leader and organized the Mormon group at the mines who planned to leave for Salt Lake. He believed a more southerly route could be opened up to Salt Lake by using the pass by which Fremont entered California four years before (1844), known as Carson Pass. This route had not been tried as an outlet from California up to this time.

Hunt had never seen the terrain and knew little of the hardship and suffering of Fremont's men and of Kit Carson's determination in negotiating the pass. This "pathfinder of Mormonism" was fearless and accustomed to hard knocks. He knew the battalion was hardened to mountain travel. A rendezvous was established about ten miles from what would soon bear the realistic name of Hangtown (present Placerville). The Mormons gave the area that they camped in the name of Pleasant Valley. They built a large corral, bought horses, wagons, and began assembling a cavalard (band of loose stock driven along by emigrant trains). A second corral was built to the north on Weber Creek. *Brooklyn* men, as well as battalion men, prepared for the unexplored trip. Gold was discovered at this place, but it did not deter these staunch religionists

from their journey. They were well-organized and ready
to start in June of 1848, but the Sierra snows had not
thawed as yet. The tragedy of the Donner Party in the
winter of 1846-47 made that pass unthinkable.

The gathering at the Pleasant Valley rendezvous had
been slow. One by one, wagons and men drifted into the
valley. Married men were discouraged from bringing
women and children where there was no road. "Wait until
we open the road," men of experience wisely cautioned.
One woman, a bride, went however. On the morning of
July 3, 1848, the wagons, with their seeds, bulbs, and supplies for the hazardous trip pulled out of Pleasant Valley.

"As the wagons rolled up the divide between the
American and Cosumnes (rivers) their brass cannon
thundered independence before the high Sierra," H. H.
Bancroft writes. This was undoubtedly the first Fourth of
July salute fired in the Sierra Nevadas. Historian Bancroft
continues: "At the call of what they deemed duty these
devotees of their religion unhesitatingly laid down their
wealth-winning implements, turned their backs on what all
the world was just then making ready with hot haste and
mustered strength to grasp at and struggle for. They
marched through new trails and new dangers to meet their
exiled brethren in the desert."

The route over the Sierras was treacherous. Few, if
any, wheeled vehicles had attempted the perilous trip. It
looked dubious to those who less than two years before cut
a road to the Pacific. They tackled the long western slope
of the beautiful but cruel mountains. Mount Talac and her
sister peaks in dazzling, perpetual snow crowns looked
down in regal scorn. Blue haze filled deep, cavernous valleys. The range was like a solid rock bastion guarding what
lay beyond. The wagons jerked and thumped up formidable grades only to drop into nearly bottomless ravines. The
horses lathered and steamed. Men of experience knew
when to help turn the wheels and when to block the wheels

to keep the load from toppling over or crushing the teams.
Captain Jefferson Hunt had cautioned, wisely, "It will be
tough going, but it can be done."

There is a tradition that the wagons were pulled up a
very high mountain—it seemed the top could never be
reached. When they looked back at the steep grade below,
they knew it would be dangerous to attempt to back-track.
They kept climbing. At last they reached the summit; below them stretched a beautiful, peaceful valley. They felt
their faith was rewarded. They named the place Hope
Valley.

The greatest tragedy of the entire journey happened
not far from that place. Captain Hunt sent scouts ahead
to explore, blaze trees, and to mark the trail. Trees were
felled to fill gullies and build ramps against mountain faces
or smooth escarpments. The road was to be permanent.
Sometimes scouts became impatient, when waiting for the
lumbering wagons to catch up, and these riders had gone
too far ahead for their own safety. Three ex-battalion men,
Ezra Allen, Daniel Browett, and Henderson Cox rode along
blazing the trail. All springs were marked. Suddenly the
three were ambushed, murdered, and thrown into a shal-
low grave near a spring. This was just over the Amador
County line in El Dorado County. The place still bears
the name Tragedy Springs. The emigrants held a funeral
service and buried their bodies beneath a tree. On the
tree they carved the inscription:

> To the Memory
> of
> Daniel Browett
> Ezra Allen
> and
> Henderson Cox
> Who were supposed
> To have been murdered

Memorial tree—where three Mormon Battalion men were killed by Indians.
Permission for use given by Hon. Joseph R. Knowland, Oakley *Tribune*.

And buried by Indians
On the night of the 27th
Of June 1848.

This site was monumented later by the Native Sons of the Golden West in 1921. In later years, when the tree fell, the part bearing the inscription was cut out of the tree and placed in the Pioneer Museum at Sutter's Fort, Sacramento, California.

Saddened and more cautious, the little caravan moved on to great heights, where the blue valley lay in beauty behind and before them, with the knowledge that another ridge must be crossed in the chill of perennial winter at high altitudes, devoid of trees, where Mountain Misery (Chamaebatia) spreads its mat of ground-clinging branches and oozes a viscid sap which inhibited and tortured both man and beast as it slowed their rate of traveling. Tediously, they moved on until, at last, the slit in the mountains discovered by Fremont's guide, Kit Carson, and named for him (Carson Pass) gave a glimpse of the purple slopes on the Sierra's eastern ramparts. The lofty Sierras would soon fall behind them as they traveled onward and eastward to "Zion."

A new type of danger and terrain were still to be dealt with. Their teams showed the strain of the ordeal, so when they reached the sloping tableland they established a resting place. A station was established here within a year, known as "Mormon Station," the first white settlement in what is now Nevada. After leaving the station, they traveled but a short distance, when they were faced by the desert. Thirst and scorching winds dehydrated them as they made their way through the parched wastes. The water of the Humboldt was alkaline, and the pools of the summer-stagnant Carson Sink were lethal. Indians were hostile, sullen, and quick with the arrow. Indian arrows felled many of their loose stock. Try as they did to watch for Indian snipers, the furtive Indians, lying on the ground, blended into the landscape like wary lizards. One waterless desert they crossed was almost a hundred miles in length. Animals became insane and unmanageable. The men's desiccated bodies were wracked by fever, and they raved in delirium. The woman suffered the least, although she was pregnant.

The emigrants swung up to the California-Fort Hall trail and went down into the Salt Lake settlement by way of Ogden, arriving about the first of October. All seventeen wagons arrived safely. The dusty caravan was little impressed by the year old settlement in the barren Salt Lake Valley. The sunset on the inland salten sea tinged the snow-capped mountains, which girdled the valley, gave a feeling of peace and seclusion. Still, however, there was something harsh and elemental about the scene. With nostalgic grief someone asked, "Can this ever be made a Nauvoo? Is this the Canaan President Young promised when we enlisted?"

Yet, it was a city of refuge. Much had happened in the two years, since they had been separated from the main body of the church. The *Brooklyn* Saints had dropped anchor at Yerba Buena Cove the day before the battalion left Fort Leavenworth. The exiled emigrants had established Winter Quarters which still served as a place of rest and protection for migrating Mormons. The battalion had cut a wagon road from the outpost of civilization to the broad Pacific; the war with Mexico had been won, and more than 595,000 square miles had been added to the territorial boundaries of the United States. While the volunteers had taught the Californians to burn brick, they had in return learned how to make adobe. These returning soldiers also brought back the knowledge of irrigation, an art of the ancient Americans, to the Mormons settling in the arid Salt Lake Valley.

The vanguard dammed a creek, irrigated land, and

planted potatoes a few days after reaching the Salt Lake
Valley. Thus, irrigation was initiated among Anglo-Saxon
people in modern times. The establishment of settlements
in the Great Basin was the parent-cell of the intermountain commonwealth. It was also the beginning of the great
colonization of the Church in the West. The loyalty of the
Church to the government was proved. The battalion was
asked to re-enlist, and they were also asked to raise a second Mormon Battalion for the army of occupation, but both
requests were declined.

In *California History*, Volume Five, Bancroft quotes
a message from Military Governor Mason of California,
written to Washington, D. C.: "Of services of the Mormon
Battalion, of their patience, subordination and good conduct, you have already heard; and I take great pleasure in
adding that as a body of men they have religiously respected the rights and feelings of these conquered people, and
not a syllable of complaint has reached my ears of a single
insult offered or an outrage done by a Mormon Volunteer.
So high an opinion did I entertain for the battalion, and of
their special fitness for the duties now performed by the
garrisons in this country, that I made strenuous efforts to
engage their services for another year." (September 18,
1847. To the Adjutant General, United States Army,
Washington, D. C.)

The Mormon Battalion had opened a road into California. When discharged, some rode to Salt Lake Valley,
converting a trapper's trail into what soon became known
as "The Southern Route" to California. The battalion
members, together with some of the men who had arrived
on the *Brooklyn*, cut the Emigrant-Carson Road in 1848
through Carson Pass, thus opening a passage for the Argonauts, who streamed to California's gold fields in 1849.

CHAPTER IV

Mormons Who Aided the Donner Party

"Change not the highway
For a byway
E'en though it be a nighway.

This little verse of the American plains was often re-peated to the hordes of emigrants who migrated West. The western migration began in earnest in the middle of the 1800's. De Voto has called 1846 "a year of decision in western expansion of the United States." During this year the Mormons came to California by water and by land; the Bear Flag Republic was created and died; the United States Navy exchanged the "stars and stripes" for the Mexican flag at Monterey and San Francisco, and the successful culmination of the Mexican War had added many thousands of acres to the United States.

All of the events of 1846 were not happy, however. Unwise decisions sometimes brought great tragedy. Of all the amazing stories of this vital period the story of the Donner tragedy is most appalling. Fact and fiction have blurred much of the history and literature of the American West. However, the factual account of the Donner Party stands out starkly in the pages of history.

What became known as the Donner Party made a fatal decision at The Little Sandy, near Fort Bridger, Wyoming, on July 20, 1846. They separated themselves from the Boggs emigrant train and from the one established trail.

The Donners and Reeds left Springfield, Illinois, in April of 1846 bound for California. In May they attached

themselves to the well-organized wagon train of a fur deal-
er and trapper, Lilburn Boggs, Jr., son of ex-Governor
Boggs of Missouri. The Donner and Reed families were
well-to-do, middle-class Americans. Reed built a large,
double-decked wagon, called the "Palace Pioneer Car,"
for the comfort of his ailing wife. Their domestic servants
traveled with them.

Jake and George Donner, as well as Reed, advertised
for bull-whackers, teamsters, and drivers. They expected
it to be somewhat of a health and pleasure trip. They retained their homes in Illinois, so that they could return to
them in the event that their intended business ventures
proved disappointing. Many Missourians took the same
precaution. The hired Mormons, however, who had no such
intentions, were on their way to join their brethren in the
West.

It is interesting to note that none objected to the presence of the Mormons in the train, despite the fact that
eight years before Governor Boggs had used his authority
to rid Missouri of the Mormons by issuing his infamous
order to "expel or exterminate the Mormons." His son did
not seem to hold the grudge of his father.

John Rhoads and his younger brother, Dan, who were
to figure so heroically in the rescue of the Donners, were
Mormons (as N. V. Jones' journal and Stewart's writings
reveal). Rhoads, Reacin Tucker, and others decided to
stay with Boggs and follow the trail until it forked off the
Oregon Trail near Fort Hall for California. The Donner-
Reed party took an untried trail known as the *Hastings
Cutoff.* This route went south around the Great Salt Lake,
over the desert, and swung up through the Humboldt to
Truckee Pass (now known as Donner Pass).

Lansford Hastings was an energetic man in his middle
twenties, who had the ambition of becoming the Sam
Houston of California. He had leadership, and he knew
that a vast migration would soon flood westward. Cali-

fornia was a rich plum for outside leadership. Hastings knew that the quickest way to get Americans to California would be to go out on the Oregon Trail and entice Oregon-bound emigrants to come to California. He had written his famous *Emigrant's Guide* and advertised it. After reading Fremont's account of his direct route from Salt Lake to California, through Truckee Pass, he decided to guide emigrants to California over this shorter route. He enlisted Jim Bridger and his partner, Vasquez, to help deflect traffic over the proposed trail.

Hastings was suave, self-confident, and convincing. If the Donners had ever heard the verse of the frontier which cautioned against forsaking the highway, they had forgotten it. They were plains people and were acquainted with neither the mountains nor the deserts. Saving 300 miles was something to take into consideration. Hastings did not explain the terrain, nor its dangers, to these inexperienced travelers. He had ridden horseback over the trail to meet the train; the weather had been good, and his youth minimized the hardships. Furthermore, it had been his only journey over that route. The Donner Party had women, children, and some ill and elderly people. Jim Clyman, a seasoned guide and frontiersman, advised against the new route. "Follow the established trail, it's longer, but you may get there quicker," he reasoned.

"I'm going the shorter way," said Reed. When they arrived at Fort Bridger on July 20th, twenty wagons pulled out of the main trail to follow a trail so new that their wagon tires barely rutted the earth. They had taken the advice of a man of whom they knew nothing, and had become a segment of nearly helpless humanity in a hostile universe. They organized a company with officers, and made their own rules and regulations "to take them to California by the most direct route." Reed's great "Palace Pioneer Car" lurched along with the faithful Milt Elliott driving. George Donner had been elected captain. A micro-

cosm of humanity was soon to be tested as human beings
had seldom been tested. Stripped of the veneer of civilization, courage and cowardice were revealed in the extreme; unplumbed depths of physical and mental torture
came, but there was still the will to live. There was no
suicide when life became unbearable.

Snow glistened on the formidable Wasatch Mountains, which proved more difficult to cross than the Conti-
nental Divide. After crossing many ranges the caravan
arrived at the mouth of Echo Canyon on August the third.
There they found a letter from Hastings, who had promised
to wait for them at Fort Bridger. He had started west with
the Young-Harlan Party. He promised to return and guide
them. They waited eight days, then Reed rode on horseback and overtook the Young-Harlan train. Near Salt Lake
Hastings went a short distance down the trail and pointed
out the way, but he would not return and guide the party
as he had promised.

The Donners were now on their own in unfamiliar
country. Reed explored routes, blazed trees, and sought
the best terrain. Trees had to be felled, underbrush
cleared, rocks removed, tree trunks piled by steep mountain sides, and at times the teams had to be increased to
eight or ten yoke of oxen hitched to one wagon to climb the
steep, rugged mountains. At other times they dropped into
ravines too narrow for the wagons or came upon narrow
trails skirting raging rivers. There were times when they
spent a week or more clearing tremendous obstacles out of
their path, only to find their way blocked again by forbid-
ding mountain ridges.

A smaller train containing the F. W. Graves and Fosdick families, as well as a single man named Snyder, joined
the Donners. This gave fresh man power, and every man
in this group made history. Finally, the pass in the Wasatch Range, known as Big Mountain or Reed-Donner Pass,
was reached. Over this historic pass Brigham Young and

his vanguard of Mormon Pioneers entered the valley one year later.

The historic Reed-Donner Pass, which had cost so much in sweat, blood, and tears, stands as a monument to the few doing so much for the many. It served the canvas caravans for almost a quarter of a century, until the railroad came in 1869. Through it came a continual train of Mormon converts, who conquered the desert and made it bloom. The Argonauts, stampeding for the California gold fields, streamed over this pass. The tragic handcart companies of 1856 came that way. A year later, Johnston's untriumphant army entered the Salt Lake Valley by this route. The thirty days of excruciating labor, almost beyond the endurance of man and beast, were a lasting blessing to those who followed. Yet, their agony cannot be described as they watched summer vanish and autumn's tints deepen on the Wasatch Mountains. This delay, where they had traveled twenty miles in twenty-six days, sealed their doom.

George Albert Smith said, "But for the success of the Donner Party blazing a road . . . into the mountains in 1846, which cost them thirty days . . . the Mormon Pioneers might not have reached the Valley early enough to plant potatoes." Brigham Young and his vanguard party came over the pass in four days. The sacrifice and suffering of the Donner Party thus proved a blessing to the Mormons a year later. When the Mormon Church built the "This Is the Place" Monument in 1947, they placed a bronze tablet, made by Mahonri Young, in grateful remembrance to the Donners, whose tire marks guided Brigham Young's party over the pass, down the canyon, and into the valley.

When the Wasatch clicked behind the Donners like a steel trap, ill-luck and misfortune dogged their every step. There were death; loss of wagons on the salt desert; loss of cattle when, thirst-crazed, they stampeded or when Indians stole them; and the agony of seeing the days and rations getting shorter. There was murder and banishment, suspicion and disharmony. Starvation stared them in the face. C. T. Stanton rode over the Sierras and returned to the straggling, struggling emigrants with food and two Indian guides. This was in late October, near the present Wadsworth, Nevada. Their oxen began dying from overwork and lack of food. Finally, they stopped to rest the cattle at Truckee Meadows. Almost immediately, angry clouds began dropping snow on the Sierras.

By October 31st, almost a month earlier than usual, the winter storms settled over the mountains. Relentlessly, they piled layer after layer of snow, obliterating the highway and pass. The dizzy precipices reared in menacing formation, blocking their way. It was the end of the road for most of the Donner Party.

There were many futile attempts to cross the mountain. With the exception of George and Jake Donner, who had been unable to get beyond Alder Creek, all the emigrants were near the lake at the foot of the pass which now bears their name. Breen, who seems to have been traveling a little ahead of the others, had moved into a cabin built by Moses Schallenberger, a seventeen-year-old boy, who had lived at the lake through the winter of 1844-45. He had been left by the Murphy-Townsend Party, because of illness, and had managed to subsist by trapping wolves and foxes.

The Donners seemed too stunned for action. By the time they realized that they must dig in and make some makeshift dwelling for the winter, many of the oxen and other cattle, which might have served for food, had been allowed to wander away and become buried under the constantly falling snow. Crowded into ill-prepared dwellings, the emigrants became gloomy and despondent. They lived on meat alone—until it was gone. Then they burned the bones and gnawed upon them. For a beverage they melted snow and made pine needle tea. Many had used ox hides to construct their sleazily built shelters. When the rations gave out, these hides were used to make a glue-like soup. Hides which had lain on the damp dirt floor were also used for food. Children were taught to cut off a strip of hide, put it on the end of a sharpened stick, hold it over the flame in the fireplace to singe off the hair, and then chew it.

Storms came in successive waves which made an almost continuous snowfall. They lived in spectral silence as the storms dumped snow to the depth of twenty-two and a half feet. (The snow was gauged later by the stumps of trees they had cut for firewood.) Cabins were constructed hastily. Kesberg's lean-to was built at the side of the Schallenberger cabin. Mrs. Murphy's shack was built at the side of protecting rock. All the other hide and brush-roofed dwellings were better than those of the aged Uncle Jake Donner and his injured brother George, a few miles away at Alder Creek. They lived in tents under a shed of pine boughs. With the oxen gone they were left in this miserable existence without transportation in the event of a thaw sometime in the dim future. There was now only one way out — to walk over the Sierras.

Among these prairie people was one who had seen mountains and winter snow. Uncle Billy (F. W.) Graves began fashioning snowshoes from oxbows which he sawed thin. He laced them in a crisscross manner with narrow strands of rawhide. The emigrants were weakened after forty-six days of privation and malnutrition at the lake, so the risk of death on the mountains' trail-less white held no more threat than the fate of possible starvation in the musty igloos which were being buried deeper by each successive storm. The young felt ready to take any risk for their parents or for their own starving children. Fifteen persons, including three young mothers, slipped on Uncle Billy's snowshoes, and set out to seek aid for those that remained behind. These adventurers were:

1. Charles T. Stanton (guide) died on trail.
2. F. W. (Uncle Billy) Graves died on trail.
3. Mary Graves (his daughter) lived.
4. Jay Fosdick died on trail.
5. Sarah Fosdick (Mrs. Jay) lived.
6. Lemwel Murphy died on trail.
7. Mrs. Harriet Pike (his sister) lived.
8. Mrs. William Foster (his sister) lived.
9. William Foster lived.
10. Antoin (a Mexican) died on trail.
11. Patrick Dolan died on trail.
12. Lewis (an Indian guide) sacrificed for food.
13. Salvador (an Indian guide) sacrificed for food.
14. Mrs. William McCutchen lived.
15. William H. Eddy lived.

These heroic people vowed "to get help, never turn back, let the future bring what it will." The first night out they camped within sight of their brethren's wretched camp. They carried limited rations: a piece of dried beef about the size of two fingers (three times a day), a little coffee, and a cube of sugar. Each had a quilt or a blanket. In addition, they had one hatchet, Foster's rifle, and some pistols. The second day they made six miles. When the sun shone, its brilliant reflection upon the snow brought snowblindness. On the morning of the fifth day Stanton sat fatigued and blind at the fire; he was so weak that he had trailed the others into camp the night before.

Mary Graves roused him. "Aren't you coming?" she encouraged. "Yes, I'm coming soon," he replied. Those were the last words he uttered to another. In May of 1847 the third relief party found what was left of his remains. Starving wild animals had devoured part of his body. Among his effects were his pistols, his torn clothing, and a poem he had written to his mother. Brave Stanton, a fine writer, and a gentleman, had crossed the Sierras twice to save the Donner Party. "Greater love hath no man than this, that a man lay down his life for his friends." (John 15:13.)

There was no guide now, except for the two Indians. A howling blizzard broke with pitiless fury. Bewildered, lost, without food, death seemed inevitable. Hunger-crazed, they remained at an improvised camp, where four of the remaining fourteen died. Insanely starved, the remaining nine stripped the flesh from their dead companions, and ate it to save their own lives. Mrs. William Foster, who from childhood had adored her brother, Lemmie Murphy, was forced to see his dead body ripped open, his heart torn out and roasted over the campfire on a long stick. Demoniacal eyes glared unseeing into space, then the heart was gulped to prolong the life of one who would later suffer a similar fate.

No group of human beings was ever forced to undergo greater torture. Finally, the two faithful Indians were sacrificed for food. Foster had become hopelessly insane. Fosdick's death was the eighth and the last. The two men and five women struggled on. They ate the rawhide from their snowshoes and the shoes and boots of their dead companions. When they got down to where grass was growing, they began eating grass.

Eddy seems to have retained his sanity, as did the women. Aimlessly wandering, they accidentally stumbled across some human footprints which led them to an Indian village. The kindly Indians anxiously ministered to them and then took them to an American settlement known as Johnson's Ranch near present Marysville. Here some emigrants had squatted four months earlier to winter after crossing the Sierras. Of the "Forlorn Hope" the snow shoe party of ten men and five women, who had left the lake thirty days earlier, only two men and five women had survived; eight men had died, and seven men's remains had been eaten by their companions. This is, perhaps, the greatest of all tragedies of American pioneering.

California sprang into action. The aroused citizens at Johnson's Ranch took the initiative. First an appeal must be made to Captain John A. Sutter at his baronial estate at Sutter's Fort for men, food, blankets, and other necessary supplies. Sutter was renowned for his generosity and sympathy. From there runners must be sent to Yerba Buena (San Francisco). The kind people at Johnson's Ranch were poor, under-supplied, recent arrivals in California, so there was little that they could do to help.

Heavy rains had caused the rivers to overflow their channels, and the plain between Johnson's and Sutter's Fort was a vast quagmire, "yet one man volunteered to speed to Sacramento with the tale of horror and get men and provisions. That man was John Rhoads (a Mormon who had come to California in the Boggs train October 29, three months earlier)."

Lashing two pine logs together with rawhides, and forming them into a raft, John Rhoads crossed the Bear River. Taking his shoes in his hands, and rolling his pants up above his knees, he started on foot through water that was frequently from one to three feet deep. Sometime during the night he reached the fort. It is said that this run took about two days.

Indian runners were dispatched from Sutter's Fort to Yerba Buena, and also to a settlement near Napa. California was sparsely settled, but these settlements went into immediate action. The people at Johnson's Ranch began grinding grain in their small coffee mills to make bread and flour; at Sutter's cattle were killed, the beef was jerked, and the rawhide was stripped to make snowshoes.

Yerba Buena was largely military and Mormon in population. Brannan's newspaper, *The California Star*, published the plight of the Donner Party. The following excerpts from that paper show the fervor of the campaign to help the snowbound emigrants:

California Star, January 16, 1847

"Emigrants on the Mountains"

"It is not probably generally known to the people that there is now in the California mountains, in a most distressing situation, a party of emigrants from the United States, who were prevented from crossing the mountains by an early and heavy fall of snow. The party consists of sixty persons, men, women, and children. They were almost entirely out of provisions when they reached the foot of the mountains, and but for the timely succor afforded them by Captain J. A. Sutter, one of the most humane and liberal men in California, they must have perished in a few days. Captain Sutter, as soon as he ascertained their situation, sent five mules loaded with provisions for them. A second party was dispatched with provisions for them, but they found the mountains impassable in consequence of the snow. We hope that our citizens will do something for the relief of these unfortunate people." The people were dismayed.

On February 6, 1847, *The California Star* announced:

Public Meeting

"It will be recollected that in a previous number of this paper, we called the attention of our citizens to the situation of a company of unfortunate emigrants now in the California mountains. For the purpose of making their situation more fully known to the people, and of adopting measures for their relief, a public meeting has been called by the Honorable A. Bartlett Alcalde of this town, on Wednesday last. The citizens generally attended, and in a very short time $800.00 was subscribed for the purpose of providing provisions, clothing, mules and horses to bring the emigrants in . . . no doubt $500.00 or $600.00 more will be raised. This speaks well for Yerba Buena."

Sam Brannan, and others, then canvassed the settlement, and contacted all ships lying in the Bay. A week later *The California Star* announced that "the citizens of this place (Yerba Buena) had subscribed $1,500 for relief of the emigrants to be expended on such articles as they may need." McCutchen raised $500.00 in Napa and Sonoma, and General Vallejo promised $500.00 to an old scout, Caleb Greenwood, if he would conduct the relief party over the Sierras to the emigrants. Like many trappers, Greenwood was a braggart. When he arrived at the snow line, he suddenly developed a case of snow blindness.

Selim E. Woodworth, Passed Midshipman, U. S. N. was given full charge of the money raised for relief. He was expected to follow the first two relief parties over the pass with food for the rapidly dying emigrants. Reed and his men awaited him anxiously. In final desperation, men with their feet split open from frostbite tramped forth to meet Woodworth and obtain food.

Woodworth had camped at Mule Springs, in Bear Valley; he never went as far as Summit Valley, although he later claimed to have managed the rescue. When the group, which was soon dubbed the *Valiant Seven*, who brought out the first emigrants from the "Lake," they found Woodworth camped on snow-less ground. Woodworth claimed to have frostbitten feet. Figuratively, he had "cold feet." Mrs. Reed and Virginia offered to care for him. A keg of fourth-proof brandy was near at hand, for the son of the author of "The Old Oaken Bucket," did not confine himself to the beverage celebrated in the song.

The conscientious people at Johnson's Ranch organized quickly to receive supplies and divide their depleted larder. Volunteers were difficult to obtain, because the war had brought a shortage of men. First to enlist was John Rhoads. He was followed by his brother, Dan, Quilla Glover, R. P. Tucker, George Tucker, R. S. Moultry, Foster (sometimes called "Sells"), Adolph Brueheim, Coffeemier (like Foster, a "ship jumper"), "Col." M. D. Richie, James Curtis, William H. Eddy, and William Coon. On or about February 4th they left Johnson's for the Camp of Death at the lake.

Soon a torrential rain fell. As the days passed the prolonged storm changed to snow. Swollen rivers were filled to overflowing by raging streams almost as wide as the rivers. It was difficult to follow the main stream—their only guide. They crossed streams on fallen logs, and dragged their unwilling horses through the muck.

A crisis never made a hero; it exposes him, just as it does the coward. Richie, Curtis, George Tucker, Billy Coon, Adolph Brueheim, and Eddy turned back. Eddy and George Tucker were weak and ill. Nevertheless, the seven, John Rhoads, Dan Rhoads, Glover, Reasin R. P. (Dan) Tucker, Sept. Moultry, Ned Coffeemier, and Joe (Sells) Foster stuck it out. After two weeks they finally faced the pass.

A mile away, and 500 feet below them, lay the camp of death, silent and lifeless to all appearances. Slowly, they began the dangerous descent. No sign of life could be seen, when they arrived at the camp. Then, slowly, a creature crawled painfully from a hole in the snow. Soon other emaciated people appeared. They were reduced to mere skeletons with sunken eyes and ghastly, demoniacal stares. The emigrants appeared too stunned and weak to speak. Finally, a woman managed to ask, "Are you from California or from heaven? We have looked and prayed so long."

The rescue party rationed out the limited amount of food that they had been able to carry over the mountains. John Rhoads, Tucker, and Moultry went to the tents of the Donners on Alder Creek with food and the assurance that another relief party was on its way. These courageous men expected Woodworth and the heralded old Greenwood to follow them in with more men and supplies. Perhaps it was best for their morale that they did not know that Woodworth had stopped at the snow line. The return trip must be made immediately as a storm threatened on the horizon. Just who was to go and who was to stay was a terrible decision which had to be made quickly.

John Rhoads had witnessed Harriet Pike's anguish as she grieved for her two babies that she had left with her mother, Mrs. Murphy, at the lake when she had left to get help for them. Her grief had touched Rhoads deeply, and he had promised to bring her babies back to her, if he had to tie them on his back.

He ran down the snow, chopped steps into the gloomy, dark cabin with its fireplace against the great rock. Dimly, he could see the distraught, blind woman kneeling at a heap of pine boughs where Landrum Murphy, her twelve-year-old son, lay in the delirium of death. "Where are Mrs. Pike's children?" he asked.

"Miz Pike's least one died night a'for last. I fed it pine needle tea and the rawhide soup we all eat. The poor little thing got so it couldn't keep the stuff on its stomach, and it died here on my lap." Then she called, "Pikie, Pikie, come to grandma. This man a-going to take you out yonder to your mama. We'll all be there soon. He says more men and food is coming." The wind started howling as she spoke. Mrs. Murphy crawled back to the side of her dying boy.

John Rhoads quickly rolled the unkempt, damp, two-year-old waif into a blanket, and hastened up the snow ramp to overtake the departing party with its 22 emigrants. The day was February 22, 1847.

Amongst the emigrants returning with Rhoads and his party was an Englishman, John Denton. He was very weak and often lagged behind. One night Rhoads went back to find him. He had traveled as far as Summit Valley and then had fallen asleep beside the trail. John Rhoads roused him and brought him into camp. Denton deeply appreciated Rhoads' kindness, but he asked his companions to make a fire and let him rest until the incoming party came to get him. The storm was becoming more and more threatening, so the party had to leave him there. The Reed Party, the second party, found him dead, still sitting where his fire had been, still wrapped in Tucker's quilt.

There in the Sierra snow fields amidst the silence of the white winter his memory reverted to the pastoral green fields of England, and he wrote a poem in a little black book with a stubby pencil. Erasures and re-written words prove his thoughts were on his writing as the sleep of death eased him into eternity. The poem follows:

"Oh! after many roving years
How sweet it is to come
Back to the dwelling place of youth,
Our first and dearest home;
And turn away our weary eyes
From proud ambition's towers,
And wander in those summer fields
The scenes of boyhood hours.

"But I am changed since last I gazed
Upon the tranquil scene,
And sat beneath the old witch elm,
That shades the village green,
And watched my boat upon the brook—
It was a regal galley—
And sighed not for the joys of earth
Beyond the happy valley.

"I wish I could once more recall
That bright and blissful joy,
And summon to my weary heart
The feeling of a boy.
But now on scenes of past delight

> I look, and feel no pleasure,
> As misers on the bed of death
> Gaze coldly on their treasure."

The seven men now goaded the emigrants on with the promise of food caches further down the trail. They sang the call of an old quadrille—a popular dance of the time:

> "Old Dan Tucker came to town
> Saluting the ladies all around
> First on his right and then on his left
> Then with the one that he loves the best."

(Now grand right and left) the extra man, Dan Tucker, got into the dance, grabbed his partner, and the man who lost his partner became Dan Tucker. The call continues:

> "Everyone look out for Old Dan Tucker
> He's too late to get his supper,
> Supper's all gone and breakfast is on cooking,
> And Old Dan Tucker is standing there
>   a'looking."

The brave men of the first rescue party cheered, sang, and promised the famished emigrants on over the pass. They expected to find the first cache in Summit Valley. Their hearts sank when they came to where the cache had been— hungry animals, coming out of hibernation, had gnawed the thongs which tied it to the branches and eaten it. The next cache was four days travel by foot into Bear Valley. Dan Rhoads, Sept. Moultry, Sells, and Coffeemier went on ahead to fetch food from the Bear Valley cache for the plodding, hungry emigrants. They ate the rawhide lacing from their snowshoes. Eight-year-old Patty Reed and her three-year-old brother were sent back to the cabins at the lake. Others died, besides Denton. Many had frozen feet, and the feet of some were splitting open, which made walking slow and excruciating. Still they struggled on. John Rhoads often broke trail with tiny Naomi Pike tied to his back.

Various writers have designated different ones as the leader, John Rhoads, Tucker, Moultry, or Glover. All of these men had been energetic in organizing and participating in the first rescue party. Yet, like most enterprises of the early West, they were a group of equals. They were seven men risking their own lives to save lives. Sheriff George McKinstry said, "They were seven men against death and on the pages of history their names should be written in gold."

Dan Rhoads, who later wrote an account of the event entitled *Rescue of the Donner Party* (Bancroft Library), claimed it was John Rhoads who blazed the trail by burning dead trees and building such other landmarks which the snows and swollen streams could not obliterate. That John Rhoads was a man of sincere conscience and quick sympathy was attested to by the young widow, Harriet Pike, whose child he brought out on the first relief party. He never wavered in his determination to bring the baby to her mother.

The men sent to Bear Valley returned with food for their comrades. They reported rapid thawing at the lower levels. When within one day's travel to Bear Valley, they met a second rescue party led by Reed, which was heading over the Sierras to bring out the other survivors.

There was plenty of food at Mule Springs. One emigrant, William Hook, died from overeating, although all were carefully watched. Horses were provided to take them to Sutter's Fort or to Johnson's Ranch. The Sacramento Valley had burst into semi-tropical March vegetation and flowers. Mrs. Reed could never forget, nor at first believe, that a few miles could effect such miracles. More unbelievable was the hospitality of the people.

John Rhoads carried Naomi in a blanket, even after

riding horses were obtained. The child was too emaciated and frail to sit alone. He must have felt a thrill and a heart tug when he placed her in her mother's arms, and full payment when the mother said, "Thank God you kept your word."

The ninth and last winter storm broke with unleashed fury and entrapped the second rescue party. Some refused to travel through it. Some did and made it to Mule Springs. A third rescue party was dispatched to bring back those at the lake that the second party would not be able to bring. Among this third party was Howard Oakley, a Mormon from Yerba Buena, who had come to California on the *Brooklyn.* This party found the remains of C. T. Stanton, who had died while leading the Forlorn Hope snowshoers out of the snow-entombed valley. Among his effects was a poem that he had written sometime during that fateful winter. Dedicated to his mother, it reads:

"To My Mother in Heaven"

"Oh, how that word my soul inspires
With holy, fond, and pure desires!
Maternal love, how bright the flame;
For wealth of worlds I'd not profane,
Nor idly breathe thy sacred name,
    My Mother.

"Thy sacred spirit dwells on high.
How oft I weep, how oft I sigh
Whene'er I think of bygone time,
Thy smile of love which once was mine
That looked so heavenly divine,
    My Mother.

"Thy warning voice in prayers of love
Ascending to the throne above

With tones of eloquence so rife
Have turned my thoughts from worldly strife
And cheered me through my wayward life,
    My Mother.

"When death shall close my sad career
And I shall before my God appear—
There to receive his last decree—
My only prayer there will be
Forever, there, to remain with thee,
    My Mother."

No history of this tragedy has ever been written which omits the story of the Patty (Martha) Reed, nor is this account complete without it. Patty, the eight-year-old, survived the terrible storm which took the lives of so many at Summit Valley. Patty was brought into Mule Springs more dead than alive, but with the resilience of childhood she bounced back to life and happiness. Unknown to all, she had carried a little wooden doll inside her little dress all the way from Illinois. This little doll had been her companion and confidante. Tied in the skirt of her petticoat was a fragment of blue, figured lawn, and folded in the lawn was a curl of her beloved grandmother Keys' silver hair. Mrs. Keys was the first death in the Donner Party. She had been buried on the Blue River back on the prairies. Also tied in the petticoat was a tiny glass salt cellar, its bowl not as large as a hummingbird's nest. Unmindful of others about her in the tent, Patty confided her gratitude for the deliverance of her treasures to her doll. There were few souvenirs of the Donner Tragedy at the lake and its vicinity, because of the wisdom of General Stephen Kearney.

After Commodore Sloat seized the California ports and hoisted the nation's flag, he appointed Captain John C. Fremont as commander of the armed forces in California.

This was not within his authority. At that time there were no Chiefs of Staff. General Kearney of the United Army had full command of the army, and managed the campaign in California from the moment that war had been declared (May 13, 1846). Thus ensued the previously mentioned dispute between General Kearney and Captain Fremont. Kearney placed Fremont under military arrest. Fremont demanded to be tried in Washington, D. C. Therefore, Kearney and Fremont each started the cross-continent trip to the national capital, with his own military escort, on horseback. Donner Pass was snow-free when they passed over it on June 21, 1847.

The thaw revealed the most ghastly sight that human eyes had ever beheld. Beloved dead, who had once been tearfully buried in the snow, had later been disinterred in a mad frenzy of hunger, and the snow-refrigerated flesh eaten by those who had once laid it away. Skulls had been sawed open for "brain tissue"; abdomens had been ripped open for the "liver and lights"; and both human and animal bones had been crushed for the marrow. It was such an appalling and revolting sight that it made even the most hardened retch.

General Kearney called a halt and ordered Major Thomas Swords to detail men to gather every fragment of evidence of the horrible tragedy, every bone, whether animal or human, and bury it in a pit in the cabin with the big rock. That done, they were to throw dry timber on all the cabins and burn them to the ground. The bodies of George Donner and some others found nearby were buried at Alder Creek. He planned to leave no shred of evidence. The grisly mess at the lake was destroyed in the funeral pyre of Mrs. Murphy's cabin.

Elder Nathaniel V. Jones, of Company "D" of the Mormon Battalion, was chosen for Kearney's escort. He kept a day-to-day journal of his march from Fort Leavenworth on July 16, 1846, to San Diego and back to Fort Leavenworth on August 22, 1847. He received $8.60 for the extra service. Jones' entry of June 21st reads, "This day General Kearney called a halt and detailed men to bury some emigrants who were overtaken by snow storms last fall. Many died . . . others lived by eating their dead companions. . . . There are dead bodies or parts of bodies lying on the ground . . . often we saw bones of the dead which had been sawed or broken open for the marrow. We set fire to the cabins. . . . A mile or more away (actually about six miles) General Kearney ordered that the dead there be buried. Also Captain Fremont passed by us at this place — did not stop."

Elder Samuel Brannan also passed the place, and, in true newspaper fashion, gave the information to the world as he rode east to meet Brigham Young, and pilot him to California.

Most of the evidence of the tragedy was destroyed at Mrs. Murphy's cabin. However, many 49ers picked up relics along the trail and swore that they had belonged to the Donners. The long and painstaking research of Dr. Walter M. Stookey, of Grantsville, Utah, covered the journey of the ill-fated Donner Party from where they left the Oregon Trail near Fort Bridger to where they lost some of their wagons on Salt Desert. There he found the remains of Reed's "Prairie Palace Car." Historians believe these remnants to be authentic.

In April of 1847 John Rhoads, Tucker, and Fallon made their last trip to Donner Lake at the request of Governor Hull in an attempt to go through the Donner tents (at Alder Creek) and bring back what property remained for the orphans. All California was filled with sympathy for the survivors. From officialdom down to the kindly peon, they opened their hearts, purses, and homes to the refugees. The brave men who performed the herculean task of rescuing the emigrants did not consider themselves heroes, nor were they so honored.

Naomi Pike as a child was carried over Sierran Snows by John Rhoads from Donner Lake to Sacramento in 1847. She lived to be 93 years of age.

Almost a year later, California was suddenly awakened from its long dream of seclusion and serenity by the discovery of gold. This proved to be the most world-shaking, history-making event in the nineteenth century. A tidal wave of humanity engulfed the state. Many individuals are remembered for their valiant actions during the opening of the new country. Yet none surpassed John Rhoads in heroism.

In 1879, thirty years after the Donner Tragedy, Judge C. F. McGlashan of Truckee wrote his *History of the Donner Party*. He contacted all living survivors. In reply to his letter Naomi Pike Schenek (then 35 years old) wrote: "I owe my life to the kind heart of John Rhoads (then dead thirteen years). His sympathies were aroused for my mother. He felt that she was deserving of some relic of all she left, when she started with the snowshoe party in search of help. He carried me in a blanket."

Judge McGlashan comments further on the above, "We have before spoken of this noble man's (John Rhoads) bravery in bearing news of the 'Forlorn Hope' and of the Donner Party to Sutter Fort. Here we find him again exhibiting the nobility of his nature by saving this little girl from death and starvation. He carried her on his back more than forty miles over winter snow." Naomi Pike Schenek attained the age of ninety-three, outliving John Rhoads by sixty-eight years. She was the next to the last survivor of the Donner Party, dying in 1934. Margaret Breen, an infant in Donner Party days, outlived her by one year.

At the age of eighty-eight Naomi Pike Schenek experienced the joy of seeing a memorial tablet unveiled commemorating the heroism of John Rhoads. He had lain, almost forgotten, for sixty-six years in a small cemetery at Slough House, a ghost town, sixteen miles from Sacramento, California. Beneath a patriarchal "tree of heaven" (Chinese locust), a bronze tablet on a base of polished granite was unveiled on a bland May morning. It reads:

In Memory of
John P. Rhoads
One of the Donner Relief Party
Born October 5, 1818
He carried little Naomi Pike over the Snow Clad
Mountains to Sutter's Fort
In 1847
Dedicated May 29, 1932
By
Liberty Parlor No. 213 Native Daughters of
The Golden West[1]

The other Mormons who figured in the first rescue party lived fruitful lives. Dan Rhoads went to Kings County, California, where he pioneered in agriculture, and fathered irrigation. In old age he was affectionately known as "Uncle Dan." The fine adobe he built near Lemoore, California, is now a museum and a historical landmark. Howard Oakley settled in Contra Costa County, and Nat V. Jones migrated to Utah.

---

[1]Liberty Parlor, N.D.G.W., is at Elk Grove, Sacramento County, California.

CHAPTER V

The Honorable John M. Horner

"You are only one, but you are one!" is the axiom of American individualism. John M. Horner was one of the 238 Mormons who came to California on the ship *Brooklyn*. He experienced the heights and depths of pioneer life. Of all those intrepid religious outcasts, he stands out as an individualist. He epitomized the tenets and ideals that gave the little band of colonists the faith to face the unknown.

History recorded more on Samuel Brannan, the assigned leader, who deserted the cause in less than two years, and made a meteoric spiral from rags to riches partly on the tithes of others. John Horner was one who neither received, nor accepted, a "call" from Brannan. Brannan probably respected and feared his mettle.

Horner was a farmer by experience and choice. The summer-brown, fog-draped hills of the San Francisco peninsula did not appeal to him as a place to begin an agricultural career. Almost immediately he and his bride, Elizabeth Imlay, whom he had married two weeks before the *Brooklyn* sailed, and another passenger, James Light, rode down around the Bay and up to Marsh's Landing (Antioch), where there were only four or five Anglo-Saxons. Dr. John Marsh had established himself on the east and north sides of San Francisco Bay. James Light and John M. Horner hired themselves to Dr. Marsh as share-croppers, and planted about forty acres of grain on shares.

The Horners had been deeply impressed by the fertile land, gardens, fruit trees, and melon patches of Mission San Jose at the foot of the Contra Costa Range, what is now Alameda County. The Horners saddled their horses and rode back to the mission, while waiting for the grain to ripen. The priests at the secularized mission were friendly, and told them that grain crops were marketable as Russia had bought grain before they sold their fort to Sutter in 1841. So Horner rented some land from an Indian.

When he returned to collect his share of the grain planted for Dr. Marsh, he was informed, "You have no share. The elk and antelope ate your share." Two burly Mexicans with drawn guns stood at Dr. Marsh's side as bodyguards.

Horner did not argue. He returned to the rented land he had plowed and planted near Mission San Jose. He later bought land from an Indian and built a two-room house (first home built by a white American in Alameda County. Livermore was English.) On the partitioning wall he built a chimney which served fireplaces in both rooms. No stoves were obtainable in California at that time. The window openings were small, high on the wall, and covered with coarse cloth. Great herds of loose cattle roamed the valley at that time. Sometimes these roving herds ripped the muslin-like cloth on the windows and looked in. Once, during a heavy rainstorm, a band of Indians sought shelter, and the Horners extended their hospitality. The Indians sat on the floor all night. When the morning dawned, the grateful Indians silently left, and their host and hostess never saw them again.

The year before John M. Horner sailed for California he and his brother, William Y. Horner, planted potatoes in the fertile triangles of land made by the zigzag fence on their father's farm in New Jersey. They spaded it by hand, and did the work in the evening after a full day's work on their father's farm. They harvested, and pitted a fine crop of potatoes. When John decided to leave New Jersey, he sold his share of the potato crop for five dollars. He added two dollars to this amount and bought a Colt revolver to protect himself in the wilds of California. However, he had found the natives hospitable and friendly, and there were no fearsome wild beasts in the area where he had settled. So he traded the pistol to a Mexican for a yoke of oxen, and began plowing and planting his fields.

Their first child was born in the little two-room house with its dirt floor, cloth-covered windows, and rawhide hinged door. This was the first white American child born in Alameda County. The child, born on December 26, 1847, was named William after John's companionable younger brother.

The barley, wheat, and vegetables that Horner had planted earlier in the year were completely destroyed by hordes of insects. In California, where spring begins in the fall—for autumn rains bring forth sprouts and green grass, planting begins in October, Mr. Horner was soon planting another crop. He said later, "Although I got neither dollars nor cents out of my first farming venture, I got experience which I profited by in later years." Great herds of roving cattle destroyed Horner's next crop, and, again, experience was all that could be chalked up on the balance sheet. In midsummer of 1848 the Horners went to the gold fields of Coloma and Mormon Island, but they found little gold. Yet John Horner was certain that gold could be gleaned from the fields of ripened grain.

The Horners returned to their little home on Mission Creek. Experience had taught Horner that he must fence his planted fields from the loose cattle. The nearest place to obtain fence posts and split fence rails was at Redwood Canyon, twenty-five miles away. There the Catholic Fathers had split the timbers for the lintels, beams, and floors of their first Mission San Jose half a century before.

Horner knew it would take two days to get to the timber, many days to fell and split the rails, and many more to drag them to his rich, alluvial farm land. He fenced sixteen acres at first. It has been said that these first fences cost a thousand dollars a mile to build. Then he bought and fenced more land. The friendly priests at Mission San Jose had proved that figs, olives, pears, grapes, and many other fruits of fine flavor could grow in abundance, if one was willing to work hard. Tall tales were told of Alviso's high wheat which he sold to the Russians.

John M. Horner continued to buy and fence land. His fences were planned to leave wide roads, where only trails had existed before. He straightened and shortened the trails by building bridges. It is to his credit that these roads still serve Alameda County after 110 years.

The discovery of gold in California had brought to its shores a tremendous and sudden population. This created an acute food shortage. Potatoes, grain, and other foodstuffs were shipped in from South America, Hawaii, and the Orient. The abundant game and wild life of California was soon killed off from ground squirrels to grizzly bears. Some species, like the valley elk, became almost entirely extinct. Horner fenced, plowed, and planted more land, despite his many failures. In September of 1849 he sold his first watermelon for two dollars.

The news spread like wildfire among the scurvied miners. "A Yankee" farmer near Mission San Jose was raising fruit and vegetables and selling them for the same price as imported stuff. Yes, sir! Onions were only $40.00 a hundred, potatoes were selling at $150.00 per ton, tomatoes at $300.00 a ton, cabbage at a dollar a head, and melons and vegetables were just as cheap. Teams came from the "diggin's" two hundred miles away to buy from John M. Horner of Mission Creek. He wrote back to New Jersey for his brother William to come to California. William was taken into partnership at the beginning of 1850.

The Horners' gross sales soon rose to $8,000.00. They bought, fenced, and planted more land; they bought teams, machinery, and put tenants on their land. Often they bought what the tenant farmers produced or sold it on a commission basis. Besides the Horners, there were few farmers in California in those days.

Many of the *Brooklyn* Mormons, ex-Mormon Battalion men, and other Americans were encouraged by the Horners to move into what would some day be Southern Alameda County. They gave them the use of land, teams, and machinery, and sold their produce on commission. At the end of 1850 Horner's gross sales were $150,000.00. By the end of 1851 the gross sales were $270,000.00. Their purchase, expansion, and development of land had been continuous. The land they bought near the mouth of Alameda Creek in 1851 proved to be an excellent investment, and the cost of fencing had become less expensive because of roads and bridges. They increased their wheat acreage. Soon they built the first steam-driven flourmill, an eight run burr, at Union City to handle their grain and that of others. Union City was authorized a post office on November 3, 1851 — the third post office in Alameda County.

The fantastic prices of the gold rush shortage were passing, but Horner had demonstrated that agricultural products could be raised in California profitably. California was gradually becoming conscious of the wealth which could be garnered by farming its rich soil in a climate which was a farmer's dream. In 1852 the San Francisco *Whig and Advertiser* announced: "Berford and Co. will carry by express today several cases of hermetically sealed samples of California grain. Among which are stalks 10 feet, 3 inches high; heads 22 to 28 inches in length; also wheat products of single grain containing 70 spears containing 4,200 grains." (Westvaco, Digest 1942.)

It was not long before the Horners bought the first steamboat to ply on San Francisco Bay, the *Union*. This ferry ran daily from Union City (now Alvarado) to San Francisco with vegetables and foodstuff for "the City." They bought a deserted ship, ran it onto the beach on San Francisco's waterfront, and converted it into a produce

market and commission warehouse. From their warehouse
and wharf at Union City they ran a stage depot connecting their stage line from San Jose with the passenger service
on their steamboat to San Francisco.

An entry from the journal of Louisa Barnes Pratt (Mrs.
Addison Pratt) describes a trip on Horner's steamboat in
the following words: "August 1 (1851), I went on board
the Union, had a pleasant passage and came to anchor (at
Union City) about 9 p.m. Remained on board all night.
I had my little Island boy with me. (Mrs. Pratt had recently arrived in San Francisco from Tahiti, where she had been
serving a Mormon mission.) The passengers admired this
little boy. In the morning I took the stage to Bro. Horner's,
where I found my daughter Frances (who worked there)
the life of the house. After a short visit there with Frances,
she came with me to the residence of Bro. Nichols—I visited
with the Tonkins at their residence; I met Brother Grouard.
I then visited Sister Stark, and Brother Stark brought me to
the steamer (at Union City) in his carriage. I have been
treated with great hospitality—The steamer set out at
3 a.m. and anchored at San Francisco about 9 a.m. that
morning."

Another entry in Mrs. Pratt's journal records the occasion of bringing the remains of a dead child from San
Francisco to be buried at Centerville. The first non-Catholic cemetery in Alameda County was given by John M.
Horner. After Horner lost his possessions in the depression
of 1854-59, the cemetery was obliterated by a grass fire, and
it has become known as "the lost graveyard of Centerville."
Mrs. Pratt also wrote of Southern Alameda County, "Such
beautiful farming country is seldom seen."*

The first agricultural fair in California was held in San
Francisco in 1852. John M. Horner was the largest contrib-
utor, and received the highest awards, amongst which was

---

*Carter, Kate, "Journal of Louisa Barnes Pratt," *Heart Throbs of the West*,
April 1947—Lesson pamphlet.

a silver goblet. While he won trophies at other fairs, he treasured this goblet throughout his life. Later, he received a letter from Professor Shelton, who had sponsored the exhibit:

"John M. Horner, Esquire:

"Although you were recently presented with the accompanying testimonial of public appreciation for your efforts to develop the agricultural resources of California, yet, I cannot refrain from adding my individual congratulations to those so universally accorded by our fellow citizens; if it be but to assure you that I heartily participate in them, and fully recognize your right to the title of pioneer, in this branch of public industry. Sir, it is true that the premium was not awarded by me personally, nor by those who could be influenced by any preferences I may have indicated, but I have the consciousness of knowing that Messers Fremont, King, Snyder, and Daunders whose pleasing duty it was to select the most worthy of the candidates for the honor, did nothing more than echo the public voice in presenting you with this goblet. Take it, Sir, no less as the evidence of public esteem, than as proof of my individual regard; keep it as a memento of successful enterprise, and as a pledge of private friendship. And, believe that no member of your family, however remote, may be his generation from our own, but will recognize it as an honorable token of the worth of his ancestor, with more pride and pleasure.

"Sir very truly
Your friend and obedient servant,
A. G. Shelton
San Francisco, California, 30th March, 1852."

At this same fair John Horner was also given the title, *"First Farmer of California."*

The following year, 1853, the Horners greatly increased their land holdings. Their potato crop is said to have yielded 11,000 tons. They harvested 1,500 acres of grain. Their stage and steamboat passenger service was flourishing. The next year Horner again won the highest honors in agricultural exhibits: a silver pitcher for the best flour, a $25.00 goblet for the best vegetables, and many lesser awards.

The irregular land laws of California caused Horner much trouble and necessitated payment many times on the same parcels of land. These land grants from Spanish and Mexican governors were very vague in outline. Sometimes Mexican governors revoked land grants and gave them to other people. Also, while the law of secularization reduced the mission lands to church property only, the priests still believed that they owned their expansive, unmarked, and undefined land grants. Deeds often read in such words as "land to extend from the dead tree to the high hill" or "as far as the sweep of the human eye." One deed stated, "this distance shall be the time it takes a man to smoke three cigars while riding a horse at normal speed."

Horner's greatest loss up to this time had been through squatters. These land grabbers usually squatted on improved land near a growing or potential town. The practice was so common that the first name for San Leandro was *Squatter's Town.* The civic-minded John Horner was the founder of most of the eight towns started in Southern Alameda between 1847 and 1854—Union City, Centerville, New Haven (first county seat), Irvington, Newark, and others.

The Horners bought 1,900 acres of land near Union City for which they paid $58,000. (Many of Alameda County's first industries were born here.) They owned $9,000 worth of real estate in Santa Clara County. In addition, they bought 5,250 acres of land adjoining San Francisco, and spent $8,000 improving it and surveying it for subdivision; the land, itself, cost $85,000.00. This, plus $18,000.00 for the steamboat, *Union,* and $85,000.00 for the mill, made quite an investment. They also owned many farmhouses, buildings, a blacksmith shop, and a wheel-wright shop. These latter shops were the first, and for some time, the only shops of this sort in Alameda County as their labor and maintenance costs were high in those days.

Horner was the first to introduce improved farming methods, machinery, and power-driven farm implements which speeded the production and reduced the costs of labor. With Beard he bought the first combined harvester and reaper in California. Shipped around the "Horn," the harvester went into use in 1854. Horner remodeled the machine, so that the thirty mules or horses which had pulled it, pushed it. This improvement saved both damage to crops and loss of life from runaways, often caused by rat-tlesnakes, disturbed hornet nests, etc. Many times envious or ignorant persons burned Horner's combined harvesters. Later issues of the *California Farmer* carried Horner's offer of free demonstrations of the machine's efficiency, and cash awards were offered for the apprehension and conviction of persons guilty of setting fire to the combined harvester.

While Samuel Brannan is often credited with being California's first millionaire, the assets of John M. Horner and Company must have totaled close to a million dollars in the early 1850's.

Yet, Horner's trusting Christian nature made him an easy touch for unfortunate or crafty borrowers. He en-dorsed many notes, and lent much money on unsound security or to dishonest people . . . he never knew how many. The first financial depression in California struck without warning; it was as devastating as an earthquake and tidal wave combined. Avaricious money lenders took their pound of flesh and the skin and blood went with it. Increased interest rates made self-help impossible. Farm products rotted in the fields; men begged, starved, or com-mitted suicide on city streets. Private capital was hoarded or used for usury. Smaller money lenders were squeezed dry by usurers with more capital than they. It made little difference that the U. S. Mint in San Francisco was grinding out just as much money as usual. Property was sold for taxes or abandoned.

Horner's crops were not sold in 1854. No one had the money to buy them—even potatoes at ten cents a bushel. Notes that he had endorsed were collected to the last penny. He lost everything, including his home, his carriage, and the watch from his pocket. Loss of his health and the loss at birth of his only daughter, Lillie Ann Horner, followed closely the loss of his possessions. Horner rented his old homestead on Mission Creek, and began again with his bare hands.

Blaming our private currency system for such financial panics, Horner wrote: "How cruel of our Congress to leave the country subject to the curse of money panics." He also wrote: "No power, but the Supreme Being, can weigh the suffering of the human heart." One of his most valuable contributions to the world was a book, *Finance and Public Money*, in which he masterfully treats the subject of private money, its use and abuse. With it all, he was an individualist. He wrote: "Don't be afraid to work yourself to death. Rust consumes faster than labor wears."

Horner was ever mindful of his humble beginning. He had amassed an estate worth nearly a million dollars by honest work and business acumen in a pioneer country. Yet he never oppressed anyone. He neither boasted nor apologized for his humble origin. His advice to young men was, "Young man, husband your present wealth of physical, mental, and moral strength; don't destroy it or waste it by smoking or chewing (tobacco); drinking, gambling, idleness, or any other dissipation. To gratify these evil habits will consume your time, health, strength of mind and body; and your acquired wealth. When you gratify them long enough—you will become a self made pauper, of no value to yourself or to the world. The wealth above referred to is subduing the earth and making it yield up its treasure to us."

John M. Horner regained his health and began working with his hands—building bridges and doing other hard work. He thanked God for his comeback. He wrote: "Not for these only am I thankful, but as in the case of Job, I have been blessed again with reasonable wealth, and an influence beyond my most ambitious hopes; and at last, though not least, have been blessed with more sons and daughters."

At the age of fifty-eight John M. Horner left California as he had come on a chartered ship. The Horners went to Hawaii, where Mr. Horner had obtained a position with the Spreckles sugar cane industries. In time Horner built up an agricultural business of his own in Hawaii. The Horners with their grown sons were an unbeatable team. It was not long before John M. Horner's influence for good was felt throughout the island kingdom. He was elected to the upper house (The House of Nobles) in the constitutional monarchy.

On one occasion, when the king was banqueting the members of the legislature, the king addressed him personally, saying, "Mr. John M. Horner, I look upon you as the champion temperance advocate of my kingdom; continue to write; it does good. I enjoy every word you write." To him the Word of Wisdom was a vital, workable instrument. When F. Hall Higgins visited Horner's only living daughter (Mrs. Josephine H. Blacow) in 1952, she recalled during the interview that her father allowed no gambling, drinking, or smoking in the bunk houses that he maintained for his hired help.

After twenty-eight successful years in the Hawaiian Islands, Mr. Horner died in his 86th year. He left a wealth of good works and fond memories in California which can well be recounted at this point.

The other Mormons who had settled near Horner in Alameda County at his invitation held cottage meetings at the homes of members. Horner rode among them as a home missionary. He read the first marriage ceremony in Niles at the Naile adobe. This was located on land now occupied by the Michael Overaker home in Niles.

There is an amusing account of how John Conrad Naile, ex-Mormon Battalion soldier, came to Alameda County. He had intended leaving the gold mines of California with Jefferson Hunt in the summer of 1848, when Hunt and his men cut the first road over the Sierra Nevadas to the Salt Lake Valley. However, he had very large feet, and was unable to obtain large enough shoes at Brannan's "Shirt Tail Store" near Sutter's Fort. He came to San Francisco to get fit. While in San Francisco, he met John M. Horner, who invited him to come to Washington Corners (now Irvington) for a visit. Naile came, and, impressed by the fertile land, stayed. He soon bought (or built) a fine adobe house. It was the scene of many social gatherings; school was held there; and the Mormons held regular church services in the attic until 1850. John M. Horner built the first non-Catholic chapel in the county of Centerville (incidentally the first Mormon meetinghouse in California.)

This was the first schoolhouse in the community where school was taught in English. After twelve years the school was moved to Irvington where it was again the first school of its type in the area. Elder Harvey Green was the first teacher at both places. It was a public school, despite the fact that the Horners paid the teacher's salary. In 1873 the building was sold, and became a part of the Powell home. This historic building, built on the present site of the Centerville depot, has a most unique history. John M. Horner, a Mormon elder, preached to a congregation of forty or more Mormons every Sunday afternoon. On alternate Sundays, the generous, broad-minded John Horner

The Horner School Schoolhouse, meetinghouse, and social hall—Built by Elder John M. Horner, 1850—First schoolhouse where English was taught in Alameda County, also first non-Catholic church in county. First Mormon meetinghouse in California.

gave the Presbyterians and the Methodists the privilege of conducting their religious services. The original congregations of these denominations were organized in Alameda County in the chapel-schoolhouse. Horner also held Mormon services at the Brooklyn Hotel in Union.

A. Milton Musser wrote of John M. Horner's support to the missionaries, "At a special conference of the Church in Salt Lake City in August 1852 there were over one hundred elders called on missions in the United States, Canada, Europe, and the Orient. We were practically stranded at San Francisco. We were to travel without purse or scrip. An ocean lay between us and our destination. . . . Elder John M. Horner who was one of the *Brooklyn* emigrants came promptly to our relief. He sent us word to ascertain what the cost of transportation would be to our fields of labor. . . . Our total cost was $6,250; of this sum collectively we had $750.00, leaving a total of $5,500.00. Brother Horner voluntarily furnished the $5,500.00." (*Improvement Era*, April and May, 1951.)

Mormon missionaries sometimes return from this volunteer service in acute financial circumstances. Jane E. Hunter's manuscript at the de Young Museum, Golden Gate Park, San Francisco, tells of Horner's and Mowry's help when her father returned after fulfilling a church mission in the Sandwich Islands in 1851. She writes: "Mr. Mowry got us a house on Market Street. Mr. Horner, another Mormon who came on the *Brooklyn*, gave father the privilege of digging potatoes on his farm near Mission San Jose. The potatoes sold at fair profit in San Francisco." She says further, "Mr. Horner loaned my father land on which to plant grain and teams to work the land, also the use of machinery—even a threshing machine. Mr. Mowry loaned us $250.00 when we later moved to San Bernardino."

In the 1856 edition of *Wilford Woodruff's Journal*, published by M. F. Cowley, there is an entry recording Elder Woodruff's account of a general conference held by the Church in Salt Lake City. On page 356 he writes of a

Home of John M. Horner—at Irvington, California. First white American to settle in Washington Township—built a two-room shack —1847. Came to what is now Alameda County, March, 1847. He and bride came on the ship *Brooklyn*, 1847.

recommendation of the General Authorities to "organize a stake (branch) at the Horner Ranch in California."

After George Q. Cannon returned from the Hawaiian Mission he was sent to San Francisco to publish a paper for the Church, *The Western Standard,* at 1181/2 Montgomery Street in 1856. Here he also published the first translation of the Book of Mormon in the Hawaiian language. The press had been forwarded from the Islands to John M. Horner of California.

When the Church's endorsed colony at San Bernardino was having financial difficulties and could not meet the payments on the Lugo Rancho, John M. Horner contributed. Parley P. Pratt, presiding elder for the Church in California, records the event:

"John M. Horner of Union City, Santa Clara Co., Calif. Put into my hand July 22, 1852 a certain Note showing two thousand dollars ($2,000.00 principle and some interest then due from Amasa Liman (Lyman) and C. C. Rich to said Horner, and which said Horner wishes to apply as *tything.* Said note was by me delivered to C. C. Rich to be credited to said Horner as *tything* on the books at San Bernardino and accounted for to the first presidency at G. S. (Great Salt) Lake City, Utah, Terr."

Horner remembered his friends in Utah even through the dark days of the depression. *The Deseret News,* March, 1856, reports: "John M. Horner of (Mission) near San Jose and George Q. Cannon of San Francisco have conferred a great favor upon Utah by sending cuttings of choice varieties of apple, pear, grape, gooseberry, etc. to Governor Young who will see that they are carefully treated . . . will Brothers Cannon and Horner, and others forward cuttings and young trees of choice variety by every seasonable mode of convenience?"

John M. Horner had substantial business connections in early Salt Lake City, notably a mercantile business in the old Tithing Office Building. To maintain this venture he kept trains of freight wagons busy between the Missouri River and Salt Lake City. In August of 1854 the John M. Horner and Company consisted of John M. Horner, Thomas Williams of Salt Lake City (silent partner), and William Henry Hooper of Salt Lake City. Hooper was active and became director in the Z.C.M.I. (Zion Co-operative Mercantile Institution), when it was organized six years later.

An advertisement in *The Deseret Weekly News* of September 28, 1854 seems to substantiate the claim that the Tithing Office store was really a department store, and that, through Hooper, fathered the Z.C.M.I. The advertisement reads:

"JOHN M. HORNER AND CO.

"Tithing Office Building Opposite Stake House have received per wagon train of 36 wagons an assortment of General Merchandise — 37 additional wagons are shortly expected, which will make the stock of the company the most complete ever offered to the citizens of Utah. Will be sold wholesale and retail as long as the contingencies of trade will allow.

"They respectfully submit the following catalogue as part of the large stock to the attention of the public."

Dry Goods Department	(Itemizing follows)	
Ladies Dress Trimming Dept.	"	"
Notions Department	"	"
Boots and Shoes Dept.	"	"
Hats and Caps Dept.	"	"
Clothing Dept.	"	"
Queens Ware Dept.	"	"
Hardware Dept.	"	"
Drugs and Paint Dept.	"	"
Stoves and Castings Dept.	"	"
Groceries Dept.	"	"

Soon after his conversion to Mormonism, John M. Horner was baptized in August, 1840, by Erastus Snow in Layawa Creek near his home in Monmouth, New Jersey. Three years later he went to Nauvoo, Illinois, then church headquarters, where he shook hands and conversed with Joseph Smith, the Prophet and founder of the Church. While in Nauvoo, Horner learned the bricklayer's trade. He also became interested in a movement to nominate Joseph Smith for President of the United States.

Much persecution of the Church had come from political pressure groups. The movement to nominate Joseph Smith was motivated by a desire to clarify the Mormon position on slavery and other issues, rather than by any hope for political success. When Horner returned to New Jersey, he took one thousand copies of the pamphlet, "Views of the Powers and Policies of the Government of the United States" (written by Joseph Smith.) At a meeting that he was conducting in his hometown in New Jersey, a man arose and said: "I have one reason to give why Joseph Smith will never be President of the United States. My newspaper came from Philadelphia this afternoon—it says that Joseph Smith and his brother were murdered by a mob in Carthage Jail on June 27." Silence reigned.

The crowd quietly dispersed. Horner said, "The grief and sadness in my heart was beyond the power of man to estimate."

Far from his New Jersey home, on the other side of the globe in the Hawaiian Islands, John M. Horner died. He had never lost contact with the Church and its publications. He contributed an enlightening autobiographical sketch, published by *The Improvement Era, Adventures of a Pioneer*, in 1904. In 1905 he contributed *Looking Backward;* and in 1906 *Voyage of the Brooklyn.*

Unveiling of John M. Horner Plaque on grounds at Centerville Chapel, October 25, 1958. Mrs. Edna Horner Matthiesen, granddaughter of John M. Horner; Elizabeth Horner Howe, granddaughter of John M. Horner.

News of his death came to President Joseph F. Smith in a communication from Horner's son, Albert, in 1907. It reads:

"Joseph F. Smith
"My dear Sir:
    "In looking over Father's papers the other day I found some interesting letters which he had received from you and your predecessors in office, and other high officials in your Church covering a period of over a half a century. Believing from these that you are and have been interested in his well being, I take the liberty of informing you of his death which occurred on the 14th of May, current year, at the age of 85 years and 11 months.

"Signed
A. Horner"

    It seems fitting to conclude this chapter with a letter from John H. Horner to his children which shows the deepness of his faith in his chosen religion. The letter, undated, is given through the courtesy of the F. Hal Higgins private collection on John M. Horner. It reads:

"My Beloved Children:
    "Some time past I sent you a Book of Mormon. I now send to you the book of Doctrine and Covenants. These two books as well as the Bible contain the word of the Lord our Heavenly Father to you, to me, and to all the world, and it is His Will, and the desire and prayer of your earthly father, that you should strive to learn and do our Heavenly Father's will. As by so doing you will enjoy many heavenly and earthly blessings here, that otherwise you cannot reach.
    "When our earthly pilgrimage is ended, and our bodies laid to rest, if we have been obedient to His Will, as above suggested, we have a sure promise our bodies and spirits will again be united through the Resurrection—never more

to be separated—1000 years sooner than they will if the above referred to commands are trampled under foot.

"If we consider the sweetness of life here, even with all its afflictions, and our great desire to prolong and enjoy health and long life here, and the short space of time a long life here fills when compared to the endless life promised to all who are obedient to His commands, we cannot wonder why some people strive so hard to obtain it, and thereby become heirs of eternal life, as well as to enjoy a larger and a happier life here. Then again, we learn from these books that our bodies after the Resurrection will no longer (be) subject to the suffering of hunger, thirst, or death, and be always in vigorous health, intellectually and physically.

"The Bible, Book of Mormon and this book of Covenants all teach the same gospel of repentance, and baptism in water for the remission of sins, and of the Resurrection. I have shaken the hand of a man that had met, conversed with, and was ordained to preach the Gospel by the hands of resurrected beings, who had been men on earth but are now angels. Those he met had been noted men of God when on earth thousands of years ago. They all told the name they were known by on earth: Moroni, John the Baptist, Elijah, the three Apostles Peter, James, and John, etc., and they informed him separately upon their visit, of the message God had commissioned them to deliver to the world through him. Each had a separate message or ordination to deliver, and delivered them. They were written down by Joseph Smith or his scribe and are mostly to be found in this book, and should be studied and obeyed, such of them as apply to all men. These messengers had been such noted men as servants of God when on earth that He raised them from the dead to be His special messengers of Salvation to the world in the last days. Before the Book of Mormon and the book of Covenants was given to the world, we had only one witness for God; now we have three, all testifying the same truths of God and His Gospel. The first, as you know was written by prophets and men of God, living in Europe and Asia at different periods of time, from 100 years after the birth of Christ back to Moses. We call it the Jewish or Hebrew Bible, the Word of God, it being both the old and new testaments. The Book of Mormon was written by prophets and other servants of God that lived in America from 600 years before Christ, to 400 years after his crucifixion, and the latter is the Word of the Lord to us and all the world and given through the Great Prophet Joseph Smith between the years 1821 and 1844. One is as true as the other—when interpreted correctly—and was communicated to the writer by God or Angels as stated above; we now have three witnesses for God, if we will accept them. The writers of these books say we are to have two more books of like import as the three referred to, being also the word of the Lord unto all people.

"One is to be the writings of men of God who have lived at different times with the ten tribes of Israel that were led captive from Samaria into Assyria by Salanger its King. After arriving into Assyria, the prophet in the Bible tells us 'They took this council among themselves; they would go into a country where never mankind dwelt, and they went a year and a half journey up the river Euphrates, entered into a hole of the earth and the Lord shut them in.' Since then the learned world lost all traces of those tribes, hence they are called the lost tribes.

"The prophets or writers of the three books tell us they are yet in existence and in the due time of the Lord will return to Palestine their old home. They are to come down from the north country and 'mountains of ice shall flow down at their presence' etc. They are to bring a book with them containing the writings of their Prophets and wise men of the dealing of Good (God?) with that people from the time they left Palestine until their return, which book will make the fourth witness for God. The fifth will be the translation of the sealed part of the plates given to Joseph Smith by the Angel Moroni, who told him to translate only the unsealed part of the plates, as the sealed part contained sacred important matter of which the world was not worthy to receive but it should hereafter be given to it.

"Who will be honored by the Great One to receive, translate and bring this sealed record to the knowledge of the world, God only knows. When it does come it will make the fifth witness for God. From what is above written it may be plainly seen our Heavenly Father has not ceased looking after his earthly children in that he gives them testimony upon testimony as proof of his existence, knowledge and power, giving line upon line, precept upon precept, here a little and there a little to persuade all to cease to do evil, learn to do well, yielding obedience to His wishes and laws by repenting of their sins and being baptised by emersion [immersion] in water for the remission of their sins, and thus prepare themselves to receive His promised blessing here, and a resurrection and life eternal in the world to come.

"Your loving
Father"
(John M. Horner)

CHAPTER VI

The Mormons and Death Valley

OUT YONDER

Yonder in the mountain's gray beauty
Wealth and fame decay;
Yonder, the sands of the desert,
Yonder, the salt of the sea,
Yonder, the fiery furnace,
Yonder, the bones of our friends,
Yonder, the old and the young
Lie scattered along the way.

—Anonymous survivor of the
Death Valley tragedy

"If all wagons follow South over the Williams Trail I'll go even if it takes us to hell," said Jefferson Hunt, the Mormon guide. "I cannot go on as your guide for I know nothing of the proposed cut off. I had never heard of it until Smith and his horseback men overtook us. I have been through the California ranges, north and south, and they are plenty dangerous, full of deep canyons and holes you may never get a wagon out of if you once get in," argued Hunt. He stood on a wind-swept knoll, his feet apart, a bull whip coiled in his hand. The wind blew his slouch hat back from his forehead, giving him a look of defiance.

"Look here, Mormon," said one with a pronounced Southern accent, "We hired you and paid you in Mormon

Money.[1] It's worthless out here and so are you. We have a good map, we'll follow that. We are on our own, and I reckon we'll get there before you." A murmur of satisfaction rumbled through the camp. They had quarreled with Hunt or each other ever since they had left the Mormon settlement in the Salt Lake Valley.

William Lewis Manly, a young, unmarried man returned from carving the date high on a rock, sat silent as the grim-faced men quarreled with their guide. The men bent their heads over the dirty map which was breaking at its creases, and satisfied themselves that this was the place where the Williams Cutoff left the main trail. Weary women took their share of recently shot dressed rabbits, and crept into their covered wagons to bury their weathered faces in their greasy aprons and cry. They feared the new trail. Manly agreed with Captain Hunt that it was dangerous to take women and children over an untried trail. The hard, wind-swept ground beneath their feet showed no mark of wagon tire ever turning off before, nor were there hoof marks of horses or oxen. Because of the desolation of the place, the emigrants named it Mount Misery.

Manly anxiously awaited his friend Bennett's decision; his belongings were in Bennett's wagon, so he would be forced to go with him. The Bennetts turned off on the Williams Cutoff. Manly lifted his reins and followed, little suspecting the tragedy ahead. He had no inkling, of course, that his part in the crisis which was to follow would make him one of the greatest heroes in the American West, and that he would some day vindicate Hunt of the blame for the Death Valley Tragedy.

Captain Jefferson Hunt was employed by some California-bound emigrants late in 1849 to pilot them from Salt Lake settlement to California. He was long criticised and

---

[1]The Mormon Church received gold dust in trade and from the tithes of California members, and coined its own $5 gold pieces, a practice permitted at that time.

blamed for the Death Valley Tragedy. The people of Salt Lake were accused of retaliatory, vindictive motives in advising the emigrants, who reached Salt Lake late in the autumn, of the danger of attempting to cross the Truckee (Donner) Pass, where the Donner Party had suffered such tragedy three years before.

Many of these emigrants were from Missouri and Illinois, the states from which the Mormons had been dispossessed, driven by mobs, and their leaders martyred. The Mormons did not know the origins of the emigrants, but the travelers did, of course, and thus feared to establish winter quarters at Salt Lake. Also, they had sufficient supplies to see them through to California, but, should the winter be unusually long, these provisions would not last. Salt Lake settlement in '49 was only an island in the wilderness. Work was scarce, supplies there were not too abundant; and the Mormons were clannish.

William Lewis Manly, the hero of Death Valley, exonerates both Hunt and the Mormon people in his book, *Death Valley in '49*. He dramatically portrays the incident of the emigrants leaving the established trail over which Hunt was hired to guide them, and going on an untried course known only on paper. They deserted Hunt! The book gives many interesting sidelights on Salt Lake and its people from the viewpoint of an open-minded observer. Manly, together with John Rogers, rescued the Bennett-Arcane Party. He is the only one to suffer the agony of thirst, hunger, dehydrating heat of the desert sun, to cross the hazardous terrain twice to keep his promise to his friends, and leave a written record. *Death Valley in '49* was written forty-five years after Manly's harrowing experience, eleven years before his death, at the mature age of seventy-four. He sought no sensationalism, nor did he seem to regard himself as a hero.

Manly recounts of Captain Hunt, "He knew more of the Southern Route than anyone else." Captain Jefferson

Hunt had been an officer in the Mormon Battalion. After he was discharged from the army he went to Utah in October, 1847, only to return to California within a short time for cattle, horses, and supplies. As previously mentioned, he guided the first wagon train from California to Utah in 1848 over the Carson Pass and Emigrant Trail.

Hunt, with the sanction of Church Authorities, was planning to take some Mormons to an agricultural colony the Church expected to promote near San Bernardino, California. He had been over the southern trail himself, but he had never driven a wagon towards California over the route. The emigrants interviewed him. It was agreed that, should the emigrant train go to California by this route, a good road would be broken between Salt Lake and their San Bernardino outpost. Hunt could be paid in Mormon money that the emigrants had earned in Salt Lake but which would not be specie elsewhere. In addition, the Mormons would gain a road to California which would be open all seasons. Never again, they thought, would emigrant tragedies, such as that of the Donners, occur. Thus, Hunt was engaged to guide the train at ten dollars per wagon, payable in "Mormon Gold."

William Lewis Manly and his friend Bennett with whom he had trapped in the West were drawn into the California gold stampede in 1849. Bennett, who had a wife and three children, drove an ox-drawn wagon and carried Manly's trunk. Manly, with five other young men, rode ahead on horseback. They planned to meet in California.

When these impatient young men reached the Green River, they were told that it was possible to float down that river until it emptied into the Pacific Ocean. They sold their saddle horses and bought boats. After floating only a short distance, they lost their boats in the swift current. Nearly losing their lives, they were rescued by friendly Indians who took them to their Chief Walker.

Chief Walker inquired, "You Mormonee? You Mormonee?" He pointed to some trinkets and said, "Mormon-ee giff, Mormonee giff." The men could see that the chief respected the Mormons and that it might be to their advantage to pretend to be Mormons. They placed their right hands over their hearts, and made an affirmative bow, saying, "We Mormonee, we Mormonee." They made it known by sign language that they wanted to go to the ocean via the river.

The chief was emphatic that the river was dangerous, too long, and ran into mountains. He told them that it would be shorter to go by way of "Mormonee" (Salt Lake Settlement), showing them also how many "sleeps" (days) they would have to travel to reach "Mormonee." Then, taking a sharp stick, he sketched the route in the ground; it portrayed an accurate map. Finally, he took dry leaves, rubbed them to powder in his hands, and scattered them over the ground to illustrate that snow would soon come, and that they must leave quickly. He provided them with food. Manly says that they owed their lives to the hospitality and humane kindness of Chief Walker.

Before these men reached Salt Lake they suffered terribly from storms. Eventually, they were overtaken by wagon trains, among which was Manly's friend, Bennett. Other trains were made up of young men from Missouri, Illinois, and Arkansas. They feared and hated the Mormons, and decided to organize themselves into an anti-Mormon society called the "Jayhawkers." Married men were excluded from the organization. The "Jayhawkers" felt that they could travel more rapidly than men with families, and that they would not tarry in Salt Lake, where the Mormons might even the score with them. They feared that, if they became winterbound in Salt Lake and the Mormons did not retaliate for the Missouri persecutions, they might still refuse to sell them supplies. Also, tales of the Donner Party made them afraid of the Sierras in the winter.

The emigrant fears of the Mormons were unfounded as the Mormons proved hospitable, although their supplies were limited, and even employed the travelers. They felt uncertain of the gold slugs coined by the Mormons. Manly says this money was engraved on one side with two hands clasped in the grip of friendship and on the other side was an eye and the words, "Holiness to the Lord."

Manly pays a real tribute to the people when he says, "Mormon morals, exclusive of polygamy, are very good. I never saw a drunken man in Salt Lake City, and I heard very little profane language there. The people are industrious and seem to be happy. Their hospitality rivals that of the old Southern Planters; and their charity was equal to that of any other Christians."

When the emigrants contacted Jefferson Hunt concerning his proposed trip to Los Angeles (San Bernardino was then in Los Angeles County), he warned them that his experience was limited and that no wagons had as yet gone from Salt Lake to the Los Angeles area. He also told them that he felt that the trip could be made safely, if they followed the trail upon which he had ridden from Los Angeles. These emigrants engaged his services, and preparations for the trip began.

One hundred emigrant wagons and many men on horseback joined Hunt's caravan. Among the wagons were seven Mormon wagons bound for San Bernardino. Hunt organized the wagon train in semi-military fashion. Lead wagons were to be rotated and become last wagons after a certain number of days. This would force all to help break trail. The people were unaccustomed to regulation, however, and Hunt found them unable to give or take orders.

After a short distance the emigrants began to resent supervision, and clamored for a shorter route that some mountain men had mentioned. Hunt yielded to their demands and went with them, but the route proved impractical so they returned to the main trail. Yet the military organization was never completely regained.

Soon a mounted train overtook them which was led by a man named Smith. Smith had a map of a southern route prepared by a man named Williams. This map showed a "cutoff" by way of Walker's Pass which led to the Tulare (San Joaquin) Valley. It showed meadows (for feed) and water holes, *but it did not show the terrain.* Smith emphasized the time and miles that could be saved by the Williams Cutoff. Many were anxious to follow Smith, but some were doubtful.

As the train continued men quarreled, long friendships were broken, dissatisfaction with Hunt increased, and the country became more desert-like with every turn of the wheels. Most of the emigrants wanted to rid themselves of Hunt; they were tired, and they questioned his motives, considering him a "treacherous Mormon." Many decided to follow Smith. After all, he had a map; Hunt had nothing but his experience.

A general meeting was called before they reached the place where the Williams Cutoff was supposed to leave the trail. Hunt said, "You all know I was hired to go by way of Los Angeles, but if you *all* follow Smith I will go with you. However, if even one wagon decides to follow this trail (the Santa Fe) to Los Angeles, I am duty bound to go with that wagon. I would not advise men with women and children to risk an untried trail. I was not hired to guide you over any other trail. I don't know any more about that trail than the rest of you. If you all go, I'll go too, even if it leads to Hell. It is untried; young unencumbered men might get through. I only know the trail that I've been over. I doubt that white men have ever been over this other trail. The map does not show the *terrain,* I repeat."

The train moved on, but people became increasingly apprehensive as the desert became more barren. On the

fringe of brush a rabbit drive was held. Five hundred rabbits were killed, and they held a feast and a council meeting.

Manly writes, "When we reached the place where the
'cutoff' left the established trail, it was an anxious moment.
Team after team turned from the trail to follow the 'cutoff.'" Now and then a team drove straight ahead on the
Los Angeles trail. Hunt watched. Smith had the greater
part of the train following him. Manly continues, "I intended following Hunt. Bennett, my friend, had joined
Smith's caravan so I went with Mr. Bennett, his wife and
children. Some were very angry toward friends who stayed
with Hunt and came back to the trail and quarreled or
bribed their friends to come over to Smith's caravan." A. C.
Erkson, whom Manly quotes, says:

"Mr. Norton came back with his whip and argued with
me when I decided to follow Hunt. He then offered Mrs.
Erkson (my wife) a horse to ride if we would leave Hunt
and join the Smith Party. Our wagon was the last to go on
Smith's trail."

Manly continued, "At Mount Misery (where the train
split) I climbed a big rock and inscribed the date, November 10, 1849." The Bennett-Arcane group had left the train
on November 4th. Six days had been consumed in separat-
ing the train.

After the division was completed, Captain Hunt shook
hands with the leader of the new train, wished him God
speed and a pleasant journey, and warned that they might
find it "pretty rough." He continued on towards Los Angeles on the well-marked trail with eight wagons. The two
trains parted forever.

Before Smith's train had traveled far they reached
impassable mountains. Exploring parties were sent out
and returned with very discouraging reports of high mountains, deep canyons, no feed for the cattle, and no water.

About eighty wagons turned around and went back to the Los Angeles trail.

The twenty remaining wagons were made up of the "Jolly Jayhawkers," to whom the enthusiastic preacher, Rev. J. W. Brier, who had influenced many to leave Hunt and join Smith, had attached himself and his family; the Bennett-Arcane Party; and some "Dust Eaters." As they proceeded along their way they found the country rocky, rough, and without vegetation. Water grew scarcer every mile.

Still they drove west. What they expected to be a pass turned out to be a box canyon. Both man and beast became dispirited. They seemed to get into deeper valleys as they passed around mountains. The heat became unbearable, vegetation lessened, then disappeared altogether. Tantalizing lakes appeared only to prove taunting mirages. The oxen became too weak to lift their heads and plodded slowly on without spirit. Provisions diminished, the water supply approached the danger point, and horses and oxen died of thirst. The emigrants ate these animals' sun-dried flesh. They found themselves in a deep, narrow valley intershot with a maze of mountain knots, extinct volcanic cones, and mountain ranges with hot, deep sand banks between them.

"Death Valley," which they unfortunately discovered and named, is an abrupt trough near the California-Nevada border. It extends approximately one hundred and fifty miles in length and has a varying width of from ten to thirty miles. The valley is two hundred and eighty feet below sea level (the lowest place in the Western Hemisphere), yet, it is within sight of Mt. Whitney, 14,495 feet above sea level, the highest elevation in the United States exclusive of Alaska. Death Valley's temperature registers 130 degrees Fahrenheit in April. It is devoid of vegetation. Such water as may collect soon becomes alkaline, and the winds are hot as a blast furnace.

Manly says of Death Valley, "We found no living thing. No bird, no animal, no insect, no reptile, no dust to cover our dead. The corpses just dried up." On one occasion they ate the desiccated flesh of an ox they found dead on the trail. Manly states, "There are no words to adequately describe the agonizing, dehydrating death by thirst and starvation. The veneer of civilization is soon lost; men become primitive, savage, and dangerous. In their insane agony these emigrants felt much inclined to attribute all their troubles to the advice of the Mormons. This was especially true of the Jayhawkers who killed most of their oxen on Christmas day (1849), burned their wagons to 'jerk' the meat, put it in knapsacks and began to walk out of Death Valley. Rev. Brier and his good wife tagging along. (Mrs. Brier proved the noblest of them and outlived them all.) The emigrants said that the Mormons willfully sent them into the desert to die—that it was the Mormon plan to wipe out so many hated gentiles and (they the emigrants) wished 'deep and loud' that the Mormons might all be buried out of sight in the Great Salt Lake. They said, 'even coyotes and turkey buzzards knew better than to go out into the country where those cursed Mormons have sent us poor numbskulls.'"

The emigrants soon broke into smaller factions. It became "each for himself." After the Christmas exodus of the Jayhawkers and the Brier family, a group of eleven men struck out together in what they thought was the shortest way out. Two arrived at the mines. Years later the skeletons of the others were found scattered about what is supposed to have been their campsite. The two that lived could never be made to tell what they knew of the camp or whether they had ever been a part of it.

Quarrels were bitter, and partnerships were easily broken. An incident is related of two friends who owned a wagon. When they dissolved their partnership, they split their wagon lengthwise, thus making it impossible for either to make a cart as the rear wheel was of much greater diameter than the front wheel. Their motto was, "he who steals food will pay with his life." Of the twenty wagon group, thirteen emigrants are known to have died. However, members of the train were divided into so many factions that there is no reliable account of just how many persons there were.

The Bennetts were a family of five—father, mother, and three young children. Arcane and his wife had one baby, and there were some single men in the party. William Lewis Manly and John Rogers left the party and went two hundred and fifty miles to seek aid for their companions. They climbed the Panamint Range, leaving Death Valley behind them; crossed the Mojave Desert and the San Bernardino Range; went down to Rancho San Francisquito; and finally arrived at the San Fernando Mission. There they were given food and the opportunity of buying horses.

The hospitable Californians seemed anxious to help. Manly bought a little one-eyed mule and some horses for the women to ride out on. On their way back to Death Valley they passed the Jayhawkers, who had lost many of their members. The rescuers soon found that the distance back to the Bennett-Arcane Party was much greater than they had expected. Fearing that the emigrants might all be dead by the time they arrived, Manly took a more direct route to the valley.

After crossing high mountains, canyons, deep barrancas, and hot deserts, they reached the trough of Death Valley. The sharp rocks cut the feet of both men and beast. As a precaution, they made a cache of part of the wheat. Soon it was apparent that the horses could go no farther without water. The men unsaddled the poor creatures and left them to die. Rogers and Manly wept when the dying horses gave pleading, pitiful neighs. Yet there was little choice but to pack the patient little mule and press on.

Suddenly they were confronted by an incredibly high

mountain range. They were forced to attempt a crossing over the summit. The route of their ascent was like a great stairway, a fissure in the side of the mountain about fifty feet deep with slick, perpendicular walls. One wall of the chasm arched a quarter circle above the other. Near the crest the other side of the chasm was slick and steep. From the steep incline it made an abrupt rise of ten feet. This formed a sort of shelf, not five inches wide, in the solid rock which ran from twelve to fifteen feet, and formed an indentation in the crest of the mountain. Then there was an easy, but steep, descent to the camp where the Bennett-Arcane Party starved, prayed, and waited. This slit in the mountainside became a great waterfall when the infrequent torrential rains brought flash-floods to Death Valley. For centuries this waterfall had washed exfoliated sand from the mountaintops and sides, and deposited it at the base of the fissure.

Manly crawled over the narrow shelf on his hands and knees, clearing it of loose sand and stones. Rogers built an abutment of stones and sand to make it possible to lead the sure-footed, cautious-stepping mule to the shelf. Manly lowered a rope after he had secured it to rocks at the top, pulled up the packs of food which Rogers had secured to its end, and then dropped the rope again. Rogers tied the rope to the mule's halter and belly band, and Manly tightened the slack. The mule was then led up the abutment. She went up to the shelf, and then, slowly putting one foot down before she lifted the other, passed over the narrow shelf. They were across! After a brief rest they repacked the wise little mule, and went down the mountain to their starving friends at the water hole.

The Bennett-Arcane Party (now reduced by death and desertion to the two young couples and the four small children) prepared to leave the water hole. They made harnesses from strips of a wagon cover, and strapped packs on the backs of the oxen. The two gentlest oxen, Christian

Crump and Old Brigham, were each fitted with a harness to which was sewn a pannier for carrying a baby. The panniers were made by sewing two hickory shirts together at the tail on the back of the shirt. When spread over the oxen's back, this made an open "pocket" on each side of the ox. The sleeves were shortened to the length of the baby's leg and made strong enough so that the child could stand on his feet when tired of sitting on the oxen's back. Strong, wide strips of canvas were made into belly bands with loops attached, so that the two older children could sit on the oxen's back, hold onto the band, and slip their legs through the loops. All but eleven oxen were killed, the hides made into moccasins, and the flesh "jerked." The women put on their best clothes, left much that they loved, and started up the mountain.

The crest, or "falls," that Manly and Rogers and the one-eyed mule had crossed must now be crossed by women, children, and oxen. Loose oxen would be killed and eaten as they crossed the deserts. The chasm was dark as the overhanging arch on the upper wall permitted little sunlight to enter.

To negotiate the seemingly impossible crossing, all, people and animals, got out of the sun's glare and accustomed their eyes to the cavern's dim light. Manly took the end of a secured rope and went over the narrow ledge. He piled soft sand into a "cushion"; then the provisions, blankets, and children were lowered to him by rope. In Manly's words, "We made them comfortable at a safe distance from the sand 'cushion.'" Next, all ropes were combined to make an exceedingly strong rope. This was fastened to the oxen's horns, halter, and belly band. Then, with Bennett on one side, Arcane on the other, and John Rogers at the rear to give a good "Tennessee boost," the animal was pushed off the cliff. Manly, below, manipulated the rope so that the ox did not break either his neck or legs as he landed on the sand cushion.

The brave, mountain-wise mule obligingly jumped down to the soft sand below. Bennett and Arcane assisted their wives over the four and a half inch shelf. They kept their cheeks, the wrist and edge of the hand to the tip of the little finger, tightly pressed against the slick side of the mountain, and slipped along with their flattened palms; then they jumped to the soft sand abutment and to their babies. One of the women said afterward that she pressed so hard against the cavern's side that she skinned her cheek from the friction, but, although she was so frightened that she kept her eyes closed, her baby's screams from below forced her on.

The falls were passed, but there were other mountain ranges, deep canyons, and pitiless deserts to cross. The two dead horses were just where Manly and Rogers had left them on the trail. Also along the trail lay the dead bodies of some of their comrades who had struck out on their own much earlier. The hot, dry winds had preserved the bodies much as they were when they had fallen.

When the party reached the caches, they found them safe but inadequate. Six of the eleven oxen were killed and eaten, and moccasins were made of the hides. (Some of the meat was probably "jerked" at this time also.) The moccasins wore out in a day's walking over the sharp rocks. At the "Valley's" rim they turned and looked back at the view. Under other circumstances it might have been beautiful. Bennett meditated long, then shook his fist in defiance and shouted, "Good-bye, Death Valley!" The name has endured.

Like the Donners, these emigrants had taken a "cutoff" on their own responsibility. The Donners suffered starvation in the stupefying, immobilizing, freezing snow; the Death Valley emigrants suffered starvation and thirst in the glaring, blistering, withering heat. Experience is a cruel teacher.

The Bennett-Arcane Party suffered greatly on the desert, and it was all Roger and Manly could do to cheer them on and stimulate hope. Finally, they arrived at San Francisquito Rancho, in the San Fernando Valley, early in March, 1850. It was just four months since they had deserted Captain Hunt on the old Santa Fe-Los Angeles Trail.

Captain Hunt's eight wagons, together with the eighty wagons that forsook the "Williams Cutoff" and turned back to the established trail, arrived in Los Angeles without trouble or incident. The Mormon emigrants guided by Hunt were the nucleus from which the Mormon settlement at San Bernardino grew.

Although the Mormon settlement at San Bernardino was short-lived, it had far-reaching influence in the history of California's industrial, agricultural, and political life. San Bernardino County was created from part of the original Los Angeles County. Captain Jefferson Hunt represented that county in the California legislature for six years.

Manly tells in his book of contacting Hunt in Sacramento, when the legislature was in session, and also of calling at Hunt's San Bernardino home where he was treated with great hospitality.

Captain Hunt lived a full life as a churchman, missionary, friend, soldier, and pioneer. After the Church withdrew its people from San Bernardino, Hunt pioneered in Utah at Provo, Parowan, and Huntsville. The latter was named in his honor, and he served there many years as a bishop. He next pioneered in Idaho, where a monument was dedicated in his honor just one hundred years after he guided the first wagons over the southern route from Salt Lake to Los Angeles.

CHAPTER VII

The Tabled Petition

The discovery of gold brought to California's shores a population large enough for this pioneer land to receive statehood in 1850. There were men of every nationality, race, creed, and color. There were men of diametrically opposed views and of every stratum of society. Transplanted feuds and hates often showed their ugly faces. This condition sometimes necessitated lawless enforcement of law for the safety of the group.

Contrary to popular belief, however, there was not much crime. Criminals knew that justice was swift and that the punishment was cruel and certain. The small percentage who did yield to crime, and who suffered accordingly, has been much over-publicized in history and tradition. The law-abiding groups, larger by far, were seldom dramatized. However, the population was not unified when statehood came. California was never a territory. Thus the machinery of lawmaking and a system of courts was not in running order when the state was born.

The capital of the newly created state of California was San Jose de Guadalupe, the oldest municipality in California. One warm, breezeless day in early January, 1850, the small pueblo basked contentedly in the winter sunshine. Across the empty miles to the south, two horsemen galloped determinedly up the Monterey Trail towards the capital.

Peter H. Burnett, first governor of California, had convened the first legislature on December the 20th. It had met only to vote a holiday recess. Then all joined the townspeople in celebrating the *Fiesta de Natal and Año Nuevo*, the Christmas and Happy New Year carnival. Now they were re-assembling to get down to the grind of law-making.

The smell of lime plaster on adobe brick and of new lumber filled the unfinished state house that January morning, when Governor Burnett sat down at the kitchen table marked "Governor's Desk." Through the unwashed window he watched the riders from the Monterey Trail tie their lathered horses to the hitching post. He thought they might be prospectors who had ridden far (they looked weary and winter frowzy) who had come to have ore assayed at the juzgado (courthouse). There was an assay office there. A single hitching post served the juzgado and the new state capitol building.

The horsemen carefully lifted a badger skin from one saddlebag, then drew from the bag a flat package wrapped in buckskin. The interested governor mused aloud, "Well, it's not ore, nor even a poke of 'pay dirt,' but whatever it is it's precious to them." The two men walked up the foot-path to the capitol and came inside to the governor's desk. Burnett seated the men on the other side of the kitchen table desk and inquired, "May I be of service to you?"

"We are delegates from the State of Deseret," the older man began.

"I know of no such state," the governor replied, his brows wrinkled.

"The people of Salt Lake Valley."

"Mormon, eh?" again interrupted Burnett.

The delegate continued, "We have brought a petition praying the privilege of being included in California's Constitution *temporarily* as East California. Our people have been in the Salt Lake Valley almost three years, since 1847, but we have had neither consideration nor representation in our national capital. This is only on a temporary basis, I assure you. We are anxious to be a state in our own right."

The preceding March the Mormons had written a constitution, and in May they organized the "State of Deseret."

However, they had an insufficient population to be granted
statehood in their own right and name, despite the fact
that the migration of many converts and friends was gradually swelling the population of the Great Basin. They
were willing to sacrifice much for representation in the Federal government. At the autumn conference the church
people, who formed the majority of the population, voted
to send delegates to Monterey, California, where that state
was holding its constitutional convention, praying to be
temporarily included as East California.

The delegates had been trapped in the Sierra Nevada
Mountains by early storms. As soon as possible, they broke
trail through the snow around Lake Tahoe and proceeded
to Hangtown (Placerville). From there they rode through
heavy rain to Sutter's Fort, waded a quagmire to Tuleberg
(Stockton), and eventually arrived at Monterey only to
find that the constitutional convention had already completed its work. The seat of government for the new state
had been set up seventy-five miles to the north at San Jose.
With grim determination, the delegates retraced the long
miles back to lay their petition before the governor.

The word "Mormon" struck Peter H. Burnett with
numbing impact. He was plagued by the heterogeneous
and disunited population of his own state, and here were
the "immixable" Mormons petitioning to be added to the
crucible. Was Mormonism to cast its shadow across his
path wherever he went, regardless of time and distance?

It was almost twelve years ago in Daviess County,
Missouri, that Peter H. Burnett had shaken the hand of
Joseph Smith, the Mormon Prophet, and the other accused
churchmen who had wintered in Liberty Jail in Clay
County. When the Mormon leaders were lodged in Liberty
Jail, they immediately secured the legal services of W. A.
Doniphan and Peter H. Burnett, lawyers of Liberty, and
later of Amos Reese of Richmond, Ray County, Missouri.
Reese did not participate until after the accused were

bound over to await the circuit court session the following March in Daviess County. Doniphan withdrew from the case when it was remanded back to Daviess County.

When the circuit court convened, Peter H. Burnett became chief counsel for Joseph Smith and his companions, assisted by Reese. All of these attorneys had taken their lives in their hands, when they decided to defend the Mormons. Feeling was so intense that the lawyers were forced to carry their guns, and a group of close, trusted friends also carried guns and acted as bodyguards. After the case was placed in his hands, Burnett spent long, intimate hours with Joseph Smith preparing the defense for the accused for when the case should be called at Gallatin, Daviess County. Burnett fought hard and lost the case. He then demanded a re-trial with change of venue to Boone County. His request was granted. He surrendered the accused men to the Daviess County sheriff, and shook hands with his clients, expecting to fight on. However, the prisoners were allowed to "escape." Thereupon, Joseph Smith and his companions joined their exiled people at Quincy, Illinois. He was assassinated by a mob in 1844 at Carthage, Illinois.

Long before this time, Peter H. Burnett had migrated to the Oregon Territory. When he heard of the discovery of gold in California, he organized and led the first wagon train from Oregon to the California goldfields. He immediately plunged into politics, when he saw the possibility of statehood on the horizon, and was elected the first governor.

"So you think your Mormon people would like to be under the flag of the United States again?" bantered Burnett.

"We have always been under that flag," continued the man from Deseret. "Our homeless people carried the flag of their country across the vacant prairies. They planted that flag on a mountain peak even before they planted potatoes. Ensign Peak was one of the first names pegged into the geography of the wilderness. Our Mormon ship, *Brooklyn,* which brought the first colonists to California under the American regime, sailed under our country's flag. Our Mormon Battalion walked across two thousand miles of desert and mountains to help win 'The Upper California' for the United States."

Governor Burnett rubbed his chin and nodded affirmatively, saying, "True, but why did Brigham Young stop in the forsaken place he did, if it were not to be beyond the reach of the long arm of the law? Did his ox give out?"

"No, sir, Brigham Young knew he would be forced beyond the Rocky Mountains. Joseph Smith, the Prophet, told him our people would be driven there," said the older delegate.

"Joseph Smith was a most extraordinary man," replied Burnett, "I believe I knew him as no other man knew him. I was his lawyer in 1838 and '39. I studied him as a man, not his religion, and knew him as a man." Events that he related and later wrote of proved his statement correct.

Years before, Peter H. Burnett and a young merchant, John McDaniel, also of Liberty, went to the settlement of Far West to hear Joseph Smith preach. McDaniel had criticized Joseph Smith in a jovial mood. Burnett writes of the church, "It was a large frame building, with well arranged seats. The congregation was orderly, devout, and attentive. The ushers were most polite and efficient in handling the big crowd. They seated Burnett, McDaniel, and other strangers, where they had a complete view of all proceedings."

Burnett continues, "Joseph Smith was at least six feet tall, and weighed one hundred and eighty pounds, or more. He was thirty-two years old, I later learned. This was the summer of 1838. He was an average conversationalist. He often used too many words, but he always made his point clear. He was a vehement speaker. He certainly was no

ordinary man. He possessed the most indomitable perse-
verance and was a good judge of men. He deemed himself born to command, and *did* command. His views were
strange and striking, and his manner earnest. One could
not but be interested. There was a kind, familiar look
about him which pleased. He was courteous in discussion
and would not oppose an opponent abruptly, but had due
deference for the feelings of others. His views and illustra-
tions were his own. He had great influence on others."

After the betrayal of the Mormons at Far West, the
leaders were taken in chains to Richmond, in Ray County,
and held in an inclosure which Doniphan later called the
"Bull Pen," where they were harshly treated. Burnett's
writings continue, "while the Mormon prisoners were under
guard in Richmond the time dragged. After the short
period of five days Joseph Smith had managed to mollify
his enemies to the extent that he could move about unpro-
tected without danger. He was a strong, athletic man and
was known to have been a wrestler. The guards proposed
that he wrestle one of their men. Smith courteously refused
on the grounds that he was, now, a minister of the gospel.
The men assured Smith there would be no betting or
gambling. It was all in fun. He then consented. They
selected the best man among their number. Smith threw
him many times in succession much to the amusement of
the spectators.

"Smith had much more influence among the Mormons
than Sidney Rigdon who had a superior education, more
dignified manner, was an eloquent speaker, and made a
fine appearance. Rigdon did not possess the native intel-
lect of Smith and he lacked Smith's determination and will
power. One could see at a glance that Smith's education
was limited.

"Later that year (1838) at an election in Daviess
County, Missouri, on the fringe of civilization the rough
frontiersmen felt they owned the land notwithstanding the

Mormons had paid for it, stopped the Mormons from voting in a regular election. They resorted to force. The Mormons in small numbers retaliated by force. This local squabble triggered the most cruel of all Mormon persecutions in the state of Missouri."

The Mormon population had crowded into the city of Far West. Much violence had occurred in outlying districts. In settlements like Haun's Mill most of the male population had been killed and thrown into a well. Governor Lilburn Boggs of Missouri called out the militia. He eventually gave the orders that the "Mormons be expelled or exterminated." Peter H. Burnett and another lawyer of Liberty, W. A. Doniphan, were in the militia and went to Far West, thirty miles away. Doniphan was a general. He was well-liked and respected in military circles.

There were so many Mormons penned up in Far West that the militia feared to enter the town. General Doniphan called for volunteers to reconnoiter and draw the Mormons out into action. Peter Burnett volunteered. There was no sign of battle formation, nor preparation for retaliation. The beleaguered people thought the militia had come to protect them from the mobs.

On the evening of October 31st, a colonel, pretending to be a friend, went into the city. He told the church leaders that General Lucas requested an interview. Joseph Smith and others accompanied Colonel Hinckel gladly. They were shirt-sleeved and empty-handed. When they reached General Lucas, Colonel Hinckel said, "General Lucas, here are the prisoners I promised to bring you."

General Lucas then issued orders to General Doniphan: "Take Joseph Smith and the other prisoners into the public square at Far West and shoot them at nine o'clock tomorrow—that's orders."

"That's cold-blooded murder. I shall not obey your orders," replied Doniphan indignantly, adding, "my brigade shall march back to Liberty at eight o'clock; and if you execute these men, I will hold you responsible before an earthly tribunal, so help me God."

He immediately sought his lawyer friend, Peter H. Burnett. "Pete, Lucas has ordered me to kill the church leaders. What do you think of that?" asked Doniphan.

"Lucas is crazy. These men belong to no military organization. They've broken no military law. The army has no right to kill civilians. What did you tell him?"

"I told him I wouldn't, so help me God," replied Doniphan.

"Good! I'll stand back of you if he starts anything," pledged Burnett.

" 'So will we all,' chorused the Clay County men who had gathered 'round us,' " said Burnett. The church leaders were held as prisoners and taken into Richmond, where a farcical trial was held, and the Mormons imprisoned. Joseph Smith, Hyrum Smith (his elder brother), Sidney Rigdon, Lyman Wight, Caleb Baldwin, and Alexander McRae were committed to Liberty Jail.

Liberty Jail was the most secure prison in that part of the state. Its outer walls were made of rough, yellowish sandstone two feet thick; the inside wall was of hewn oak logs. Between the walls was a foot wide space filled with loose rock. The building measured twenty-two by twenty-two and a half feet on the outside. There were two floors. The ground floor had a small, cross-barred window in each end to give light and ventilation. It was reached by a trap door five feet by two and a half feet wide. The lower floor was usually referred to as "The Dungeon."

The accused Mormons in Liberty Jail secured Peter H. Burnett and W. A. Doniphan as counsel, along with Amos Reese, as previously stated. Burnett says, "We apprehended that we may be mobbed, our clients taken from us and hung. . . . We determined to do our duty at all hazards and to sell our lives as dearly as possible if necessary. . . . We armed ourselves and had a circle of brave faithful

Hon. Peter H. Burnett, first governor of California, who, with William A. Doniphan, another attorney of Liberty, Clay County, Missouri, defended Joseph Smith, Jr., and other Mormon leaders who were imprisoned in Liberty Jail in the winter of 1838-39. Burnett was chief counsel when case was remanded back to Daviess County. Burnett was governor when Deseret applied to be admitted to the Union as East California, 1850.

friends armed around us. Our first move was to get the accused prisoners out on a writ of habeas corpus. The proceedings were held in a small room in the second floor of the courthouse in Liberty. That limited spectators to about one hundred. Judge Turnham was firm and fearless in the discharge of his duties.

"I made the opening speech; the District Attorney replied; Doniphan made the closing argument. As he arose to speak, I whispered to him: 'Doniphan, let yourself out, my good fellow; and I will kill the first man that attacks you.' He did let himself out, in one of the most eloquent and withering speeches I ever heard. The maddened crowd foamed and gnashed their teeth, but only to make him more and more intrepid. He faced that terrible storm with the most noble courage. All the time I sat within six feet of him with my hand on my pistol, calmly determined to do as I had promised him."*

Rigdon was released. The other prisoners were remanded to await the action of the Grand Jury of Daviess County, which was to meet the following March—months later.

During that winter in Liberty Jail, Joseph Smith wrote much. He was deeply concerned for the physical and spiritual welfare of his exiled people, who had now crossed the Mississippi River to Quincy, Illinois. Some time between March 20, 1839 and the convening of the circuit court in Daviess County, Joseph Smith wrote a long letter to Bishop Partridge at Quincy. It was not intended for him personally, but "for the saints at Quincy, and those scattered abroad." It begins like ancient Hebraic poetry:

> "O, God where art Thou,
> And where is the pavilion that
> Covereth Thy hiding place?
> How long shall Thy hand be stayed

---

*Burnett dedicated his book, *Observation and Recollection of an Old Pioneer* to Doniphan.

And Thy eye, yea, Thy pure eye
Behold from the eternal heavens
The wrongs of Thy people
And of Thy servants,
And Thine ear be penetrated
With their cries?"

Sections 121 verse 1, and 122, and 123 of the Doctrine and Covenants are excerpts from this letter. Joseph Smith wrote it, signed it, and then had all his companions at Liberty Jail add their signatures.

"Late in March," wrote Burnett, "the spring term of the District Court of Daviess County was convened. We prepared to go. The sheriff of Clay County removed the prisoners under strong guard from Liberty jail, took them to Gallatin, Daviess County for the impaneling of the grand jury. It was apprehended that the prisoners may be mobbed by the irritated people of Daviess County. The sheriff was determined to protect them, also Reese and me.

"Court was held in a rough log school house, about twenty-five feet square. There was a spring thaw, and the lane, a quarter of a mile long which led to the school house, was knee deep with soft mud. Great crowds collected. Violence was feared every moment. The prisoners were seated on a long bench in one corner and guarded. In the other three corners was a fireplace, the judge's desk, and a bed for the counsel (Reese and Burnett). The floor was soon tramped hard with mud. It looked like an earthen floor. The Mormons were well aware of the danger they were in. They never slept. Reese and Burnett slept in the opposite corner. We could see all that went on. By permission, also by consent of the accused, people were allowed to interview them. Many local citizens and others, friends and enemies came to converse with the prisoners. They talked incessantly all night long, night after night. Even ministers of the gospel came to argue religion. Smith invariably silenced them sooner or later."

The Mormons were convicted on two true counts from the plethora of charges on which they were held. Burnett immediately filed for, and was granted, a re-trial with change of venue to Boone County. He then surrendered the accused to the sheriff of Daviess County, and parted from them with a friendly handshake. That was his last legal contact with Mormons, he thought. Now, as governor of California, one of his first out of state problems was an appeal from the Mormons to be temporarily included in the new state of California.

The names of Jackson County, Daviess County, Haun's Mill, Far West, and Liberty Jail were seared into the memory of every Mormon by the branding iron of experience. Governor Burnett was the first man the delegates had ever met who had been so close to it all, whose opinion had not been swayed favorably towards, or prejudiced against the Mormons.

"To reconvene California's Constitutional Convention to consider your petition is impossible," replied Governor Burnett to the pleading of the Deseret delegates. "That would make one state, East-West California, of all land ceded to the United States by the treaty of Guadalupe-Hidalgo of 1848. California has no desire to expand its borders or to annex territory. Allow me to state that I appreciate your need of representation and your loyalty to your country. I shall be glad to take your petition, and, when our crowded agenda permits, I shall lay it before the California Legislature for their consideration and vote," said the governor, arising to signal that the interview was at an end.

During the long, hectic weeks which followed, Peter H. Burnett studied Deseret's petition and the accompanying constitution. He annotated it, and wrote voluminous notes. The notes and recommendations far outnumbered the combined pages of Deseret's petition and constitution, when the governor laid it before the legislature.

The Assembly rejected the petition without an opposing vote. Tradition says that the action was taken without reading the petition. The Senate voted to table the petition. It has been tabled for one hundred and ten years.

CHAPTER VIII

San Bernardino

A deathly silence settled like a pall upon the Mormon congregation in the little meetinghouse in San Bernardino, California, one Sabbath afternoon in 1857. The ward clerk had just completed reading a communication from Brigham Young, President of the Church of Jesus Christ of Latter-day Saints. Young requested that the church colony at San Bernardino, and all church members in California, "regardless of condition, or circumstance" come to the Salt Lake Valley at once. An army under the command of Colonel Albert Sidney Johnston was marching in to lay siege on Salt Lake City. The citizenry at Salt Lake had decided to meet the invaders with a "scorched earth policy." They were willing to apply torches to their homes, rather than surrender their possessions to mobsters and invaders as they had done so many times. No one seemed to know just what had provoked the invasion.

Actually, there were several reasons why Johnston's Army was sent to occupy Utah. Utah was organized as a territory in 1850, and, for a time, the mechanism of government proceeded smoothly with Brigham Young as governor. Eventually, however, the government sent non-Mormon territorial officers to take over the reins of the territory. These territorial officers were antagonistic towards the Mormon faith, and demanded both church and personal records. The demand was refused. Many trials resulted which were presided over by a judge, who opposed polygamy, while himself outraging Mormon morals by maintaining a common law[1] wife. Rumors and colored accounts of the dissension between the Mormons and the territorial officers filtered back to Washington, D. C.

By 1857 there was already some intimation of the approaching Civil War. It was desired to place troops on the frontier in readiness for the impending conflict. Also, there is strong reason to suspect that President Buchanan's Secretary of War, Floyd, had other motives. Floyd was a Southern sympathizer and many believe that he may have desired to remove the support of these Union troops from the Union cause by sending them as far away as possible from the probable battlefields. The excuse for the occupation was the unrest among the Mormons; the actual reasons seems to have been linked with the gradually developing Civil War.

Colonel Henry Inman, Assistant Quartermaster of the United States Army, says on page 121 of his book, *The Great Salt Lake Trail*, concerning the six thousand men mobilized for the *Army of Occupation* in Utah: "They were well equipped with immense supply trains and thousands of loose cattle. When that was exhausted they were supposed to live off the people of the Territory—by forage, or otherwise. . . . The people of the territory were in a starving condition in consequence of the failure of crops and unusually severe winter of 1856-57. There were thousands who for over a year had never realized what a full meal meant; children by the hundreds endured the gnawings of hunger until hunger had become to them a second nature. Yet, despite this condition of affairs the orders issued to General Harney from Washington display lamentable ignorance, or a determination to compel the Mormons to feed the troops on the basis of the miracle of 'The loaves and the fishes' . . ."

The Mormons intercepted the army, by means of

---

[1]"Common law" adjective dignifies the woman more than she deserves. She was no wife . . . "Common law" relationship is legal *only* when the parties have legal capacity to contract a marriage. If either party is already married but undivorced, he or she is without *legal* capacity to contract another—not even—or especially *not* a common law marriage. Legally of the common law compact between the parties to live together as husband and wife, and "holding out" each other to the world as husband and wife, is legitimate *only* when parties are not under legal disability of an existing (undissolved by divorce) marriage.

guerrilla warfare, and destroyed the supply trains and
stampeded the cattle. They burned army bedding and
extra clothing. Although the Mormons had bought Fort
Bridger and built Fort Supply where the troops anticipated
spending the winter, the guerrillas burned them to the
ground. The Mormon leaders had instructed their guerrillas "to save life always—we do not wish to shed a drop
of blood if it can be avoided."

General Harney had declared, "I'm ordered to Utah
and I'll winter in the valley or in hell." However, Harney
was relieved of command for other duty in Kansas, and
Colonel Albert Sidney Johnston succeeded him in command of the troops bound for the Utah Territory. In the
severe winter of 1857-1858 these troops suffered more in
the Rocky Mountains than Washington's troops suffered
at Valley Forge. They stayed in Utah for four years.
They, and everyone else, wondered "why." The troops
called the occupation "Buchanan's Folly." At the out-
break of the "War between the States" it was obvious to
all why so many men were sent so far from Washington.
Colonel Albert Sidney Johnston transferred his command
to the next in rank in 1861, and immediately joined the
Confederate forces. He distinguished himself as a strate-
gist, and was killed in action at the battle of Shiloh, April
6, 1862.

The people at San Bernardino were heartsick. "Would
the Mormons always be driven into the wilderness, and
be expelled after they had conquered it?" "Why should
other people reap the harvest of their sowing?" "Why
should they leave the lovely San Bernardino Valley?"
They were too far away to help repel the Army, and all
had been counseled to avoid belligerency and the commit-
ting of overt acts. Yet, like Joshua of old, each knew in
his heart that he would obey.

From where they sat many could see their cozy homes,
the Lombardy poplars shimmering and scintillating in their

autumn gold, michaelmas daisies, asters, and other fall flowers blooming in their front yards, and the young orchard trees browning. All heads were bowed in aching silence. Men blew their noses to hide tears; women folded their handkerchiefs or rolled the ends of their bonnet strings. Unchecked, some teardrops splashed down on white, starched Sunday aprons. In that small group were those who had crossed the ocean in steerage, walked the limitless prairies, climbed the Rocky Mountains and descended into Salt Lake Valley, then traveled over alkali sands and cactus deserts to pioneer in the San Bernardino Valley.

Life in San Bernardino had not been easy, but nature had rewarded them. The young orchards and vineyards were coming into full bearing. Many anticipated building better homes and planting more fields. The year 1857 had yielded an abundant harvest. To leave all this meant supreme sacrifice.

Ten years before Captain Jefferson Hunt first entered the San Bernardino Valley, while exploring inland for the United States Army. He felt sure that it had unusual possibilities for colonization. After being discharged from the Army on July 16, 1847, he immediately rode horseback toward the Salt Lake Valley, where he knew the migrating Mormons expected to settle. He arrived there about a week after Brigham Young and his vanguard first struck their tents. The place seemed barren, and survival through the first winter seemed dubious.

After a council meeting, it was decided that the Mormon ex-Captain Hunt organize an expedition to return to Southern Californina to buy horses, cattle, food, and supplies. Hunt improved his trail (which later was used when a railroad was built), and entered San Bernardino by way of the old Southern Trail and the steep Cajon Pass. (He by-passed this entrance for a more gradual grade in 1851.) The Chino Rancho and the Lugo brothers in San

Bernardino sold Hunt 300 head of cattle, and 150 head of horses, and some supplies. Hunt assembled his pack train, employed local *vaqueros,* and headed back to the Salt Lake Valley. Upon completion of his mission, he returned to San Bernadino. Much of his subsequent activities have been discussed in prior pages.

After Jefferson brought the initial colonists to San Bernardino, he attempted to impress Brigham Young with the advantages of an expanded colony. President Young was apprehensive of dividing his people into far-flung, isolated areas. However, he realized that there were economic, commercial, and ecclesiastical gains to be made. Roads made by the emigrants gave outlets to Pacific ports, and church converts from countries "down under" and from the Pacific islands could stop, rest, and equip themselves for the overland journey to the Utah Territory.

In 1851 President Brigham Young acquiesced to Hunt's plan. A colonial project was organized, and the Church sponsored the colony in Southern California. Elders Charles C. Rich and Amasa M. Lyman were set apart as leaders. Soon 500 wagons assembled at the rendezvous for the trip to San Bernardino. Brigham Young was amazed at the number so willing to leave the Salt Lake Valley. He said, "I was heart-sick at the sight of many of the saints running to California chiefly for the God of this world. I was unable to address them." However, he made no attempt to stay them.

Hunt had his train organized in a semi-military manner, and led them over a road he had largely developed himself. They entered California through the Cajon Pass, six miles west of the steep route established by the Spanish explorers. The first camp in California was made at Sycamore Grove, fifteen miles from the present city of San Bernardino. Schools and temporary community life were organized, and much appreciated after three months on the dusty trail. The leaders began to explore the San Bernardino Valley for the natural resources, such as water, timber, soil, etc., and searched for a site on which they would locate a city and build homes. The Los Angeles *Star* welcomed the home seekers as "Good industrious neighbors."

The Mormons first contacted Isaac Williams and made an offer to buy Rancho del Chino. He refused their offer as being too low. They next negotiated with the Lugo brothers who owned a land grant from the Spanish government. The Lugos set the price at $77,000. The Mormons had no money, but Hunt had friends in the northern part of the state and at the mines. He went to San Francisco, contacted his friends, and was able to raise $20,000 for the down payment. Like many land grants, the Lugo grant had indefinite boundaries. After much litigation, it was found that the Lugo grant was eight leagues not the eighteen leagues that the Mormons thought they were buying. The eventual settlement of claims gave the Mormons only 35,500.4 acres. This misunderstanding caused some Mormons to settle on land which was not their own, and some gentiles to settle on church-owned land.

Men were determined to remain where they had settled, regardless of ecclesiastical affiliations or court decisions. Gentiles lined up with Mormons, and vice versa. An amusing, but at the time a bit serious, incident occurred. A man named Benson had settled on land which the court decided was "Mormon land." There was a perpetual spring on the land, which the Indians had known of and used for centuries before the white man came. After the Mission San Gabriel was founded, the Mission Fathers used the spring for watering their cattle; it was also used for baptizing their Indian converts.

There was a hard, beaten trail from the "sacred water hole" to the mission. The trail is rich in tradition. Jedediah Smith followed this trail when he went to San Gabriel in 1826; the survivors of the Death Valley tragedy were rescued over the trail in 1850. Many famished wayfarers followed the path to the mission. When the state courts decided that the spring was on land bought by the Mormons, Benson became belligerent. He threw up "earthworks" at the spring, mounted an ancient brass cannon, and was ready to do battle. However, there was no military encounter; an amicable and satisfactory settlement was arranged. Therefore, the place became known as "Fort Benson." (In later years the Native Sons and Native Daughters of San Bernardino parlors erected a historic landmark at the spring commemorating "Old Fort Benson."

The deed reconveying the Lugo's Spanish land grant to the Mormons was recorded February 7, 1851. Many colonists had chosen a site for their homes and had begun planting earlier when the autumn rains set in. Now they began surveying, and laying plans for a city, individual homes, public buildings, and roads. These activities were suddenly interrupted by rumor of an Indian uprising.

Generally, the California Indians were peaceful. However, in November, 1851, there had been a scrimmage at Warners' Ranch in San Diego. A white man was killed, and feeling ran high. The United States Army sent companies of soldiers into Southern California. A military unit was stationed at Rancho del Chino with a small arsenal for issuing ammunition to settlers for defending themselves in the case of isolated attacks from Indians. The Mormons were ordered to collect at a place where they could defend themselves and their stock. The cattle were rounded up, and driven to a place where they could be guarded. Men were sent to Rancho del Chino to draw arms and ammunition from the arsenal. Captain Jefferson Hunt was made commander-in-chief of the two Mormon divisions.

It was decided to build a fort at once, an enclosure of eight acres, large enough to hold all families. Moving of their buildings started immediately. Each man was assigned a position of work, and held responsible. The ground enclosed was in the form of a parallelogram, 300 feet wide by 720 feet. The north, south, and east sides were made of cottonwoods and willow trunks with the edges fitted tightly together. The logs were sunk three feet into the ground, and they projected twelve feet above. Log houses already constructed were moved along the west side to form a solid wall, which was finished with logs placed in blockhouse fashion. Loopholes were made, bastions built, and the gateways were indented to allow for crossfire.

Water was ditched in from Lytel Creek, and storage reservoirs were made within the enclosure. On three sides, eighteen feet from the wall, eighty-five log houses were erected for family living quarters. Additional sleeping arrangements were provided by using the wagon beds from the covered wagons which had brought them to California. A small group preferred to take their chances outside the fort, and camped on what later became the old cemetery. Many lived in the stockade for more than a year. Flora B. Huston says,[1] "Arms and ammunition were sent from Rancho del Chino, where a small garrison of United States soldiers had been stationed. Guard was kept at night and a signal system adopted—Uncle Grief, an elderly Negro who had an old horn in his possession, was to sound the alarm in case of attack. Buildings were erected within the enclosure. A combination meetinghouse, schoolhouse, and storehouse with office space, and a wagon shop served community needs. All historians feel that the fears of the settlers were justified even though there was no attack. The hastily built fort served a purpose."

San Bernardino built a $600,000 courthouse on the site of the old Mormon Council House. The day after its dedication (April 10, 1927), the Arrowhead Parlor of the Native Sons of the Golden West unveiled a bronze plaque at Sycamore Grove, where the first camp of the Mormon founders of San Bernardino was made fifty-six years before.

When the Indian trouble was settled, the Mormons

---

[1] *Touring Topics,* April, 1930. No longer printed.

resumed their community and individual projects for which lumber, adobe, and other building materials were needed. There was plenty of timber along the steep mountainsides. To less courageous pioneers this would have been impossible, but the Mormons decided to erect a sawmill in the mountains. First, however, a road must be built up the nearly perpendicular grade to the timber.

Every man in the settlement was "called" to put in his entire time and use all his teams and equipment in building the road and moving the machinery up to the sawmill. The resulting road has been pronounced by engineers as one of the greatest public works projects accomplished. It was twelve miles of road straight up a mountainside.

All men and teams stayed more than two weeks, and many put in extra time. It is estimated that the road cost 1,000 hours of man labor. It possibly went over the knoll now tunneled by the railroad to Arrowhead Hot Springs, up through Waterman Canyon, to the steep mountain a mile or a mile and a half below the summit, and then ascended the difficult pitch crossing the line of the present High Gear Road. A memorial plaque was placed at the crossing. It is made of native stones, mounted on a wagon wheel imbedded in cement, and reads, "Pioneer Monument, Marking the old Mormon Trail on High Gear Road near Crestline, California. Erected and Dedicated—Thursday Club, Crest Forest District November—1932."

After the Indian scare the people moved their houses back to their own claims. The city was laid out much after the design of Salt Lake City; there was a fort, a temple block (now Pioneer Park) schoolhouses, broad streets, and large lots for homes which provided for flower gardens and ornamental trees in front and family orchards and vegetable gardens at the rear.

The Mormons bought grist mills as well as sawmills. George Surrine, a millwright of San Francisco, was sent for. He helped Lyman and Rich select a site for and erect the first grist mill. Surrine's old crosscut saw is a lone survivor of that period of heroism and hardship. It is in case number 1355 in the museum on Temple Square, Salt Lake City, Utah. The card beside it reads: "This saw brought from New York in 1846 by George Warren Surrine to San Francisco, California (Yerba Buena) coming around Cape Horn on the old ship *Brooklyn*. The ship's log showed she had traveled twenty-four thousand miles getting to San Francisco. It went to San Bernardino, California in 1852—then to San Diego in 1856; then to Salt Lake City in 1858, then to Paris, Idaho (Bear Lake Valley in 1863); then down to Mesa, Arizona (Maricopa County) in 1877. This is the property of Warren L. Surrine's son.

"This crosscut saw was presented to the Museum on Temple Square, Salt Lake City July 26, 1937 by W. C. Surrine."

The rich soil and plentiful water brought abundant harvests to the colonists. Their flour sold in Los Angeles for $32.00 a barrel. Los Angeles was then the county seat. Cemented by religious ideals and objectives, the Mormons prospered. However, they were not pharisaical. They entered wholeheartedly into the political life of California, and worked for Jefferson Hunt, who was elected to the lower house of the state legislature. He served them there for six years.

Largely through Hunt's efforts, San Bernardino County was created in April, 1853, from the original counties of San Diego and Los Angeles. It became, and still is, the largest county in the United States, 20,157 square miles. More than ninety per cent is desert. The valley is semitropical, the mountainsides well-timbered, and the snow-capped mountains give an abundance of fresh water. The first elected and appointed city and county officers were church members as the population was predominately Mormon.

The fame of the valley spread as their farm products, cattle, and flour were exhibited at county and state fairs. Many non-Mormons filtered into the town and valley. Many of these latecomers resented seeing so many church men holding office. A political party was organized known as "The Independents." They accused the Mormons of misusing their power. At the election of 1856 much defamatory literature was printed and circulated, to no avail. The friends of the Mormons supported them wholeheartedly. All were working together for better schoolhouses, better buildings, a public library, and for home beautification. More ornamental trees and shrubs were planted. Farming and viticulture were expanded and improved. Young orchards were coming into bearing. Prosperity was apparent everywhere.

Dr. Barton and his wife were among the first non-Mormons to settle in San Bernardino. Just when they came is uncertain. They had driven an ox-drawn covered wagon from Texas to California. Dr. Barton's granddaughter, Miss Clara Barton of Piedmont, California, says that her grandfather was welcomed by the Mormons. Dr. Barton was one of the first doctors in the settlement, and he also built the first drugstore. It was across the street from the Mormon Council House, and also housed his office and the first post office in a public place. Dr. Barton was the first paid postmaster. Until that time the office had been voluntary. Dr. Barton was a devout Baptist, and his wife was a charter member of the South Methodist church; but they both loved and associated intimately with the Latter-day Saint people of San Bernardino. I quote now from personal correspondence with Miss Barton:

"Both my grandparents had sincere admiration for the Mormon people: Their courage, ability to work together, and determination to accomplish what they set out to do. Both Rich and Lyman were valued friends. Grandfather had more respect for Rich than Lyman. Grandmother said, 'It's only because you (meaning grandfather) like to argue with him over horses, orchards, crops, and everything.' It was all good naturedly, of course. Priscilla Rich, wife of Charles E. Rich, was grandmother's favorite friend. They had so much in common. They exchanged recipes, talked of their problem children, and helped each other with their sewing. When it came time for the Mormons to leave San Bernardino for Salt Lake (1857) my grandparents gave them (the Riches) a farewell party. Grandmother and 'Prissie' Rich wept on each other's shoulders as they said good-bye. I never knew whether they corresponded or not after being separated." Dr. Barton bought much church and personal property from them when the Mormons left San Bernardino.

The economic cost of the exodus has never been estimated, nor did it influence their decision. Instances had been related of a well-planted farm being exchanged for a camping outfit for the journey. Another was a four-room furnished house being sold for $40.00 with a buggy, a cloak, and a sack of sugar being thrown in for good measure. Prosperous members crowded the aged or less fortunate members into their covered wagons. Some were forced to remain, but they were promised that wagons would be sent back for them.

In the northern part of the state there was no organized plan for mass migration. The depression of 1854-1857 (California's first money famine) had struck with a suddenness and devastation which reduced many honest, ambitious men to pauperism. Many were broken in health and spirit. Although most of the Mormon men in this area rose above the situation and in time regained a measure of their pride and affluence, they did not go to Utah. For some unaccountable reason, official contact with the scattered members in California was not resumed after the army was withdrawn and the Mormons and the government were on amiable terms. Church missionaries had been called in from California and the islands of the Pacific, and the missionary system was not reactivated for thirty-five years (1857-1892).

The recall of church members to Utah from San Bernardino, California, and the islands of the Pacific ended official contact with its members in California, except for personal correspondence. Three years later, in 1860, the Reorganized Church of Jesus Christ of Latter Day Saints was organized. Their missionaries proselyted vigorously among the shepherdless flock of original Latter-day Saints in California with a high degree of success. Among them, however, were many who questioned the authority of the Reorganized Church. Alfred Nethercott wrote to Wilford Woodruff requesting that missionaries be again sent to California. This was done, and a branch of the Church was organized: the Oakland Branch at Oakland, California, on October 2, 1892 with six original members. This included San Francisco and all California.

Branch President, Joseph Natress, Oakland
First Counselor, Dr. John Peter Phillip Vandenbergh, San Francisco
Second Counselor, James Peter Jorgensen, Oakland
Branch Clerk, Norman B. Phillip, Oakland
Member, Mrs. J. P. P. Vandenbergh, San Francisco
Member, Mrs. J. P. Jorgensen, Oakland

It is a tribute to Brigham Young's influence with his people that the majority of his followers unhesitatingly forsook wealth, ease, and political leadership to comply with his request.

Southern California regretted the departure of their Mormon citizens. Many newspapers acknowledged their thrift, diligence, and miraculous accomplishments as colonizers. The Mormons were credited with having shown a wonderful faculty of conciliating the Indians. Columns were devoted to their roadbuilding, their grist mills, and their united effort in doing the seemingly impossible. Their community life and conduct had been unequaled. They were sincere in their religion, peaceful citizens, and they had no rioting, no murders, and few lawsuits. They had proved the value of small farms and diversified farming, irrigation, and a well-planned city lay as a monument to their engineering genius.

The City of San Bernardino was patterned closely after Salt Lake City. Its streets were wide, surveyed on sectional lines, and shade trees bordered them. Many houses were built of adobe with gables built of native lumber and roofs of shakes. A proposed temple block centered the city, and streets were numbered from there. Many streets bore names associated with their church leaders or events in church history. After the Mormons left the street names were changed and forgotten.

There is a tradition that the American name for Mount Palomar was once *Smith Mountain,* and that it was named for Joseph Smith, the Mormon leader. From 1859 to 1868 it is marked on California maps as Smith Mountain. In 1954 the American Trust Company published a brochure, *Colorful California Names,** which listed the original name as Smith Mountain. In 1901 the citizens petitioned to have the Spanish name, *Palomar,* restored officially. This was done.

The request to return to the Salt Lake Valley was a numbing shock to the thrifty, successful Mormons at San Bernardino. Besides their prosperous farms and other industries, good roads connected them with Los Angeles and its seaport, San Pedro; the El Camino Real to the north, the old Spanish Trail to the east, and the Southern Route to the intermountain country were further outlets for their agricultural and business ventures. It was rumored that the businessmen of San Bernardino were considering the construction of a railroad between Salt Lake City and Southern California. The loss of the Mormon citizens

---

*Brown, T. P, *Colorful California Names,* American Trust Co., 1857, p. 28.

greatly decreased the population of the county for some time. Gradually, other people drifted into the area to replace the Mormons. However, there was no longer the drive of a united community which in six years had developed a city and a county.

San Bernardino has a good right to be proud of its Mormon beginning. On June 25, 1932 The History and Landmark Committee of Lugonia Parlor, 241, Native Daughters of the Golden West, with Miss Clara Barton as research chairman, dedicated a bronze tablet, mounted on a stone shaft from the famous Doble Mine in Bear Valley (first gold mine discovered in San Bernardino County) honoring the first public building in San Bernardino, the old *Mormon Council House.* The monument was placed on Third and Arrowhead Streets, on a corner of the present courthouse plaza.

The San Bernardino *Sun,* Sunday, June 26, 1932, says, "San Bernardino honored its Mormon founders yesterday by impressive public service to dedicate a monument on the southeast corner of the courthouse grounds—site of the first public building erected in the city eighty years ago, a Marker placed by Lugonia Parlor, N.D.G.W. An address was delivered by Dr. Richard R. Lyman of Salt Lake City, Utah, a grandson of Amasa M. Lyman. Miss Naomi Rich, granddaughter of Charles C. Rich, co-founder with Lyman, was also introduced by Miss Clara Barton. After the dedication ceremonies Miss Rich and Dr. Lyman were entertained at the log cabin club house in Pioneer Park. Pioneer Park was once set aside as a site on which to build a temple. The inscription on the monument reads:

> "In memory of Charles C. Rich and Amasa M.
> Lyman, builders of this council house 1852
> —First School-Church—and later Court
> House of this county—Dedicated by
> Lugonia Parlor No. 241—

Native Daughters of the Golden West
June 25, 1932."

From church records furnished Miss Barton by Andrew Jensen she quoted: "April 3, 1852 the council house was nearly covered by all hands having been at work on it the previous day. The first public meeting was held Sunday, April 4, 1852. This was the first public meeting in San Bernardino—covering completed April 5th (Monday). Our new Council House is a commodious building.

"July 20, 1852 we erected our bowery and council house which is an adobe building with a good shingle roof —60 feet long and 30 feet wide; in which we held our April conference. It is occupied during the week by our day school—on Sundays and after services it is occupied by our Sabbath School and Bible Class."

The Mormons laid a firm foundation for building an industrial, commercial, religious, and civic life. They were remembered as progressive citizens, good neighbors, and true friends. Their colonization of San Bernardino wove a bright thread into the tapestry of winning the West.

The chapter which follows will bring us up to near modern times with the account of one of California's most gracious and talented literary figures, Ina Coolbrith, California's Poet Laureate.

CHAPTER IX

Ina Coolbrith — Josephine Donna Smith

She walks with God upon the hills
And sees, each morn, the world arise
New, bathed in light of paradise
Unveiled before His eyes, she stands
And gives her secrets to His hands.
    —Ina Coolbrith
  (Tribute to a dead sister poet)

The sudden ringing of the telephone shattered the after-hour silence in the office of Dr. Henry Meade Bland, English professor at San Jose State College. He was a prolific writer and did most of his writing at his office after classes. A gorgeous sunset tinted the campus buildings and cast a glow over the whole Santa Clara Valley — a most fitting atmosphere for his subject, an obituary for California's Poet Laureate, Ina Coolbrith, whose funeral he had recently attended. Her passing had been as vivid as the close of this sunny March day in 1928. The skull-capped English professor ignored the persistent ringing until he completed and punctuated his sentence; that done he took the phone from its cradle on his desk.

"Hello, yes, yes, yes." He sat in perplexed silence as he listened to the voice on the other end of the wire. "What? No, I did not know that Ina Coolbrith was her pen name. Nothing irregular, if it were. What! Her real name was Josephine Donna Smith? She was named for Joseph Smith, the founder of Mormonism? Please read

that over. Who wrote it? A reporter on the New York
Sun named Bob Davis?" A flicker of recollection came
into Dr. Bland's classic face. "By the way, I met a man
at Miss Coolbrith's funeral last week in Berkeley. He
claimed to be related to the late Poet Laureate. I believe
his name was Smith." With his free hand Dr. Bland
emptied his pockets on his desk. "I thought I had that
man's card with me. It must be at home. I'll look it up
and get in touch with him. He may be able to throw
some light on this Bob Davis scoop. What? You don't
believe it? Neither do I! If I get any information from
Smith, I'll call you back. Good-bye."

Ina Coolbrith was dead and literary circles everywhere
mourned her passing, especially San Francisco, the "city of
her love and her desires," which had long claimed her as
its own. She had come to the city by the Golden Gate in
her vivacious twenties, when both she and the city were
young. The literary groups enfolded her, and she helped
create its Golden Age in literature, molding many lives
which made San Francisco the marvelous reality into which
it grew, a new and throbbing tradition fashioned from all
creeds, colors, and every stratum of human society that the
discovery of gold had lured onto California's shores.

This Argonautic school had given the world the writings of such authors as Bret Harte, Charles Warren Stoddard, Mark Twain, Henry George, Prentiss Mulford, and a
whole galaxy of new stars in the world of letters, but the
girl, Ina Coolbrith, far outshown all others. She outlived
them all, and was crowned Poet Laureate of California in
1915, the first woman, indeed the first person, in America
to be so honored. Although academically untrained, she
was counselor and critic for her contemporaries. Even Bret
Harte, most fastidious and self-satisfied of all those early
writers, sought her criticism and suggestion. From her
help, Bret Harte portrayed the emotional and elemental
nature of man in a hostile environment, without coarseness

First Poet Laureate of California, First Librarian of Oakland, California, Ina Donna Coolbrith (Josephine Donna Smith), daughter of Don Carlos and Agnes Coolbrith Smith. Permission for use given by Ina Graham.

or crudity.   Ina Coolbrith urged him to publish such short
stories as *The Luck of Roarin' Camp; Outcasts of Poker
Flat,* and others which have never been surpassed.   Miller,
whom she gave the pen name of Joaquin, Stoddard, and
others, grew and blossomed under her tutelage.

When Ina Coolbrith came to San Francisco, her life
began anew.   She drew a curtain of silence between life
in San Francisco and her past.   Whatever her reason, she
kept her past from the present with true Victorian dignity.   Ina never wrote an autobiography, although friends
urged her to do so.   She laughingly replied: "Were I to
write what I know, the book would be too sensational
to print; but were I to write what I think proper, it would
be too dull to read."

Dr. Bland puzzled over the writing of Miss Coolbrith's biographical sketch.   How could he round it out
with no flashback to her parents and childhood?   Not long
before her death he had made her the subject of a column
he conducted in a local newspaper, "Autologuing with
Authors."   (Dr. Bland traveled by automobile on these
trips and called it "autologuing.")   In these little intimate
journeys to the homes of California authors, or to those who
knew them, he often discovered priceless incidents in their
life stories.   Not so with Miss Coolbrith.   Life began in
the city by the Golden Gate where she became one of the
editors of the first *Overland Magazine,* and established herself as a poet of the bright and beautiful, the lovely in
nature and life.

Dr. Bland sat down again in the silence of the deepen-
ing spring night.   He reasoned: "What if she did prefer to
live by her pen name; it implied no deception."   Pseudonyms
had been the vogue among early California writers.   Sam
Clemens was better known as "Mark Twain"; William
Wright as "Dan De Quill"; C. F. Brown as "Artemus
Ward"; Charles Warren Stoddard as "Pip Pepperpod";

Lieutenant George Derby as "John Phoenix"; Prentiss Mul-
ford as "Dogberry"; Alonzo Delano as "Old Block"; Rollin
Ridge as "Yellow Bird," his Indian name; and Cincinnatus
Hiner Miller dropped the nickname of *Hiney* Miller- for
Joaquin Miller, legalizing the latter, at the suggestion of
Ina Coolbrith.   Even Louise C. Smith signed the enlighten-
ing, descriptive letters of the mines, which she wrote to her
sister, as "Dame Shirley."

The little baby girl, who was to grow up to be known
as Ina Coolbrith, was christened Josephine Donna Smith on
March 10, 1841, at Nauvoo, Illinois, when it was the largest
city in that state.   She had two older sisters, Agnes and Sophronia; the latter died when little Donna was two years
old.   Her mother was Agnes Coolbrith, a timid, refined
convert to the church of Jesus Christ of Latter-day Saints.
She left her home in Boston, and migrated to Kirtland,
Ohio, Church headquarters.   There is no record of her family contacting her after she left home (see the book, *Mary
Bailey,* by R. Smith).   This was not an unusual happening
among early converts to Mormonism.   Lucy Mack Smith's
book records that Agnes Coolbrith and her friend
Mary Bailey both came to live with her, the Prophet's
mother. In later years, both married into the Smith family.
Agnes married Don Carlos Smith, the Prophet's youngest
brother, a literary, gifted newspaper man.   At the time of
Josephine Donna's birth he was editor and publisher of the
Times and Seasons, largest newspaper in the city and official organ of the church.

Missouri had been made a slave state by the Missouri
Compromise; its citizens had fought hard to get this ruling
from the Federal Government.   The old settlers deeply
resented the Mormon settlements on the frontier for many
reasons: they were fiercely intolerant of the "new-fangled
religion"; they were jealous of the thrifty communities the
Mormons built; and they feared the Mormons' anti-slavery

stand.   They resorted to robbing, beating, and mob violence to overthrow the Mormons.

In 1838 Agnes Coolbrith Smith was alone in her farm-
house in Daviess County, Missouri.   Suddenly, a merciless
mob drove her from her house and burned it.   She walked
three miles carrying an infant in her arms and little Agnes
on her back to get to the protection of friends.   She had to
wade Grand River, waist deep and partly frozen.   After the
robbing and mobbing at Far West, Missouri, the Mormons
were driven across the Mississippi River into Illinois.   The
winter was cold, and it was difficult to move the 1,200 destitute people.   Don Carlos Smith returned to the Missouri
side, dug up the printing press which had been buried in
the sand, set it up in his cellar, and began printing his
paper.   Mud and water oozed up between the loose planks
of the floor.

The young father developed pneumonia which left
him in a weakened condition; he died in the summer of
1841 at the age of twenty-five.   Little Sophronia died two
years later, leaving the widowed Agnes "desolate indeed,"
to quote her mother-in-law.   Within three years her father-
in-law and her three splendid brothers-in-law died. Joseph
and Hyrum were murdered at Carthage Jail, and Samuel
died within a month from grief and shock.

After completion of the Nauvoo temple,* Agnes Coolbrith Smith took her two little girls to the temple for sealing
ordinances.   She then moved to St. Louis, Missouri, and
began life again.   In 1846, when the Mormon vanguard
started west, Agnes and her children remained in St. Louis.
The children were cautioned not to tell their names.   After
some time the young widow married William Pickett, a
printer on the St. Louis *Republican.*

Shortly after Donna's eleventh birthday in 1852,
the Pickett family started for California in a covered wagon.
The beauty of the spring prairie flowers, the pre-dawn blue

---

*Smith, Ruby, *Mary Bailey,* chapter XXII, p. 105.

of the sunrise, and the evening glory of the sunsets made an everlasting imprint upon the poetic mind of the eleven-year-old girl, but, like all emigrant children, she had her responsibility. She was baby tender for her chubby three year old half-brothers, Don Carlos and William Pickett.

Through the long wearisome trip the desiccating sun shrank the wagon wheels until the tires almost fell off. In Utah the Indians were on the warpath. The worn-out oxen almost stopped in their tracks before the formidable Sierra Nevada Mountains were reached. The mountains were the last hurdle, and, since the Donner Party's tragedy, were feared and dreaded by all wagon trains.

When the Pickett train reached the abrupt incline of the Sierras, they lost the trail among the acres of sharp, broken rock, which showed no imprints of tires or ox hooves. Women wept and the men studied frantically the worn, dirty roap map. Little Donna took her brothers to play in the shade of the wagon. The children were unaware that the eyes of a home-hungry man were watching them. Jim Beckwourth, half-breed Caucasian and Negro, ex-chief of the White Chief Crow tribe, trapper and scout, exclaimed with a profane expletive, "There is the sweetest things the Good Lord ever made!" Then, touching his spurs to his horse's flanks he rode over to the men studying the frayed map, "I've found a better and lower pass a few miles to the north. No wagon's been through yet, but it's a heap safer."

The emigrants accepted his offer to guide them into California through the pass which now bears his name, "Beckwourth Pass." When they reached the gap, the old scout bent down and lifted the gray-eyed, eleven-year-old girl up on his horse, sitting her in front of the saddle, saying, "The little girl will be the first through the pass." As they glimpsed the green majesty of the Sacramento Valley, Beckwourth threw his sun-tanned, race-tinged dark hands wide apart and said, "Little Princess, there's your kingdom," bequeathing the two-year-old state of California to the child, who was to grow up with the state.

The Virginia-born half-caste, Beckwourth, who had always lived with the Indians, little knew how close his forecast came to the truth. Could he have lived another sixty-four years, he would have seen this child crowned Poet Laureate of California and his own name pegged into the map of California. He remained a hero in the heart of the poetic little girl, who rode ahead of him through the newly discovered pass in the challenging Sierra.

After the emigrants made camp, the tall pines on the sun-saturated western slope of the mountains tempted Donna and her little brothers to explore the forest. The leaping tree squirrels, swiftly running quail, and chattering blue jays enticed them far from the trail. The darkness of night settled over the forest. Willie and Donnie began to scream and cry. Donna comforted them and said, "We must keep very quiet or panthers may hear us and come to eat us. Mother says 'God watches over us wherever we are.' " The children cuddled down in the ferns and slept until dawn.

The Pickett family remained only a short time at the mines, where they found little gold but much malaria. Soon they traveled on to San Francisco where they joined an emigrant train leaving for the Mormon colony at San Bernardino. Pickett was a man of much experience and above average education. He obtained a notary public's commission and expected to handle minor legal cases. However, the colony's disputes were handled by ecclesiastical tribunal, so Pickett packed and moved to the pueblo Los Angeles, in the "valley of smokes," as the Indians called it. Here there was greater opportunity to accomplish his political and business aspirations.

California of that day had a polyglot, heterogeneous population, yet there was some prejudice and intolerance of the Mormon Church and those who may have been connected with it. Agnes Smith Pickett deemed it advisable that their relationship to the Church be kept secret. She swore her daughters to secrecy, and never released them from the vow as long as she lived.

Donna attended what is said to be the first English-speaking school in Los Angeles. She wrote and published poetry in California newspapers under the pen name of "Ina." She was tall and matured early, and her beauty and charm made her a most striking young woman. On the occasion of a great social affair, she was chosen by ex-Governor Pio Pico to lead the grand march.

On September 9, 1858, at the age of seventeen, Donna married Robert B. Carsley. She was married under her own name, Josephine Donna Smith. Carsley was a businessman and an amateur actor in local musical shows. Soon his unwarranted jealousy, ungovernable temper, and coarse, vulgar language became unbearable to the religious, refined girl. On the slightest provocation, he would fly into a rage and leave his wife, only to return later and make false accusations. Three years after their marriage he rushed from the home in a temper tantrum, and went to San Francisco for a short time. He soon returned to harass his young wife with threats, unrepeatable names, accusations of unpardonable acts, and other intimidations. Finally, he shot at her with a rifle, pointed a pistol at her and slashed at her with a carving knife.

Donna fled to the home of her kindly stepfather for protection. Mr. Pickett was cutting kindling wood when Donna arrived. Seeing that Carsley intended doing the girl bodily harm, he rushed to her rescue with his ax in hand. Infuriated, the temper-crazed Carsley turned on Mr. Pickett. In the melee which followed Carsley's right hand was injured to the extent that it had to be amputated.

Josephine D. Smith (Carsley)* was granted a divorce on grounds of extreme cruelty on December 30, 1861. Judge Benjamin Hayes commented that "the young woman had been the victim of a pathologically jealous man, who had no grounds for accusing his wife of infidelity." Carsley did not contest the divorce.

In the early 1860's the Pickett family moved to San Francisco. Ina combined her pen name and her mother's maiden name, and began life anew. The past was her own, and she imposed it on no one. Ina needed no introduction to San Francisco as she had frequently published her verse in the *Californian, New Era,* and even eastern newspapers. She was loved, honored, and respected as Miss Coolbrith. In after years Dr. E. Clarence Stedman called her "the Sappho of the Pacific Slope." Seldom did a hint of her past sorrow, and never a granule of bitterness, seep from her warm, radiant verse. She made a happy home with her parents and taught school for Professor Mirielle. Soon she established herself in San Francisco's literary and publishing circles.

There is an emotional glimpse of her past in her early San Francisco verse. Ina contributed some poems to *Poetry of the Pacific* (second book of verse published in California, compiled by May Wentworth and financed by Samuel Brannan) in 1867. One of these poems entitled "Fragments from an Unfinished Poem" follows:

Oh, balm and dew and fragrance of those nights
Of Southern splendor 'neath Southern sky!
The soft star closes to the golden days
I dreamed away in that far tropic clime,

---

*Walker, Dr. Franklin, *San Francisco's Literary Frontiers,* Pub. A. Knoph, New York 1943, chapter III, p. 57-64. "North Portal of Beckwourth Pass is Mount Ina Coolbrith."

Ibid., Reference and notes, p. 375.

Marriage and divorce, See Los Angeles Co., Marriage Certificates, Vol. I, page 22-23. For divorce, see Los Angeles District Court Case 853, Josephine D. vs. Robert B. Carsley.

Wherein Love's blossom budded, bloomed and died!
Even amid its horrors; for we clothed
Each dim surrounding object, with the hues
Of our worship—and the things else
Had seemed most darksome and unlovely were
By our great love transfigured and divine.

The following two poems breathe of disappointed romance:

Cupid Kissed Me

Seek I Love Who has taken flight
Comes no more forever:
Love from whom more pain than bliss
Every heart obtaineth.
For joy soon vanished is
While the pang remaineth
Well-a-day, ah, well-a-day!
Would Love I had missed thee.
Peace and I are twain for aye
Since Cupid kissed me.

Unrest

I cannot sleep; For morning memory apes
Her dream domain and sorrow roams the bowers
Searching amid the withered leaves and flowers,
That strew the ruined footpaths, for the hopes
That perished with them—perished utterly!
Through all my life have pain and passion wove
Their subtle network; by the grave of Love
I knelt and shed a tear.

Only in this early verse does deep sorrow or sad memories find expression. One poem, "A Mother's Grief," is thought by some biographers of the poet to reveal that she may have borne a child and lost it, during the three years she was married to Robert Carsley.*

THE MOTHER'S GRIEF

So fair the sun arose yester-morn
The mountain cliff adorning;
The golden tassels on the corn
Danced in the breath of morning:
The cool, clear streams that run before,
Such happy words were saying,
And in the open cottage door
My pretty babe was playing.
Aslant the sill a sunbeam lay.
I laughed in endless pleasure,
To see his little hand essay,
To grasp the shining treasure.
Today no shaft of golden flame
Across the sill is lying:
To-day I call my baby's name
And hear no lisped replying;
To-day—Ah, Baby mine today—
God holds thee in His keeping,
And yet I weep, as one pale ray
Breaks in upon thy sleeping.
I weep to see its shining bands
Reach with fond endeavor
To where the little restless hands
Are crossed in rest forever!

Dr. Franklin Walker's book, *San Francisco Literary Frontiers*, states: "Only in her early San Francisco writings do we glimpse the real Ina Coolbrith." I do not agree with Dr. Walker entirely. In her last book of poems, *Wings of*

---

*Dr. Franklin Walker, *San Francisco's Literary Frontiers*, Alfred Knopf, New York, 1943; p. 225.

the Sunset, which came out shortly after Miss Coolbrith's death, we find that the volume is dedicated:

> To the boy
> Carl
> Whose song
> Begun on earth
> To be finished
> In heaven.

Ina was too young to have remembered her gifted father, Don Carlos Smith, but perhaps his life had been related to her by her mother, and she honored and was proud of him as the name Carl suggests.

Ina Coolbrith turned early to nature for her lovely lyrics. Her adopted state, California, furnished her with inexhaustible inspiration. She loved the snow-thatched mountains which girded its semi-tropical valleys; its patriarchal redwood trees, summer-brown hills with lavender sunsets; its caressing fogs which enfolded one like a chiffon scarf. She watched the fleets which berthed at the city's wharves and dreamed of faraway people and places. She saw beauty in the tiniest flower, and caught the litany of the eventide bird song. Beauty and love flowed from her pen.

In 1864 Ina Coolbrith made her debut in the publishing world, when she became co-editor with Charles Stoddard and Bret Harte on the first *Overland Magazine.* Its slant was to develop the literature of the New West. It printed only original material and paid cash. Each editor carried a key to the office on the old Portsmouth Plaza. These three have long been known as "The Literary Trinity of the Golden Gate." Mark Twain, Prentiss Mulford, Joaquin Miller, and many others whose names were to glitter in Western literature, all haunted the *Overland's* office, when they were young and trying to grasp the first rung in the ladder of fame.

All of these young writers came to the tall, grey-eyed, beautiful Ina for counsel, inspiration, and encouragement. She was a most attractive, quiet, and refined woman. Joaquin Miller described her as "A daughter of the gods, divinely tall, and most divinely fair." She remained friend, critic, counselor, and companion, but she neither encouraged, nor yielded to, any amorous entreaties. The seven years on the old *Overland* were the happiest years that Ina Coolbrith had ever known, or ever would know.

She corresponded with most contemporary writers of her day. Death had taken her mother and her widowed sister. Ina assumed the responsibility of her sister's two children. Joaquin Miller "bequeathed" to her care his half-breed Indian daughter, Calia-Shasta, issue from one of his Indian marriages. The handsome Miller was leaving for a sojourn in Europe. Ina felt a pang when her friend left as she had always planned to visit Europe, its authors, its poets, and its literary shrines.

About this time, Mrs. Harriet Beecher Stowe, a natural crusader, had literally yanked Lord Byron from his grave, and opened up much scandal concerning his domestic affairs from old letters which had been brought to light. Her book, *Lady Byron Vindicated,* was much discussed over the teacups of those who thrive on scandal. Ina loved Byron's poetry. She appreciated him as one of the great romanticists, equal to Shelley, Keats, and others. England ignored Byron's contribution to the world. His remains reposed at Hucknall, Newstead Abbey, unhonored and unmarked.*

Alone, Ina Coolbrith took the ferryboat to Sausalito, then went to a laurel grove in Muir Woods and gathered a great quantity of laurel leaves. She wove a lovely laurel wreath with her own hands, and requested Joaquin Miller to go to the ruined chapel and lay the wreath

---

*Dr. Henry Meade Bland, 1828 class at San Jose State College, *Writers of the Pacific Slope;* class notes of author.

on Byron's neglected grave. Her heart sang as she composed a poem, "With a Wreath of Laurel."

Miller went to Hucknall Torkard chapel at the old abbey. He looked at the monument which Byron, when young and rebellious, had placed near the grave of his favorite dog. Miller meditated on the ways of men and wrote his poem, "In Men Whom Men Condemn as Ill."

IN MEN WHOM MEN CONDEMN AS ILL

In men whom men condemn as ill,
I find so much of goodness still,
In men whom men pronounce divine
I find so much of sin and blot,
I do not dare to draw a line
Between the two, where God has not.

The wreath and the poem of the Western poet awakened the literary world. The King of Greece sent a wreath to be placed beside the wreath Ina Coolbrith had sent. The Joaquin Miller poem was read everywhere. England began to make plans to restore the ruined abbey and the five hundred year old chapel. The project soon spread to international proportions.

After the first *Overland Magazine* suspended publication Miss Coolbrith moved to Oakland on the opposite side of San Francisco Bay. She became that city's first librarian. She served the library for twenty years (1875-1895). Ina encouraged children to use the library, and they loved her. A little wharf rat from the Brooklyn Mud Flats aroused her interest. He read voraciously, was a promising writer, and Miss Coolbrith encouraged him. This boy was Jack London. He called her "my literary mother." On one occasion, he presented her with one of his books autographed with this line: "To one who opened the gates of knowledge to me."

Isadora Duncan, the dancer, lived in Oakland as a

child. In later years she wrote in her autobiography, "The librarian in Oakland was a wonderful woman. . . . She seemed pleased when I asked for good books. . . . Her eyes glowed with burning fire and passion. In those days I ran, skipped or danced to the library. That librarian was Ina Coolbrith, the poetess."

Adults, as well as children, appreciated her help and loving service. Her years of pioneering in establishing the library were suddenly terminated, because of intra-city politics, in which neither she, nor her department, had participated. One whom she loved dearly replaced her. Ina believed in the law of compensation and eternal justice as the following poem (so loved by John Greenleaf Whittier) reveals:

WHEN THE GRASS SHALL COVER ME

When the grass shall cover me,
Head to foot where I am lying—
When not any wind that blows,
Summer-blooms nor winter snows,
Shall wake me from your sighing;
Close above me as you pass,
You will say "How true she was"
When the grass shall cover me.

When the grass shall cover me.
Holden close to earth's warm bosom—
While I laugh, or weep, or sing,
Never more for anything,
You will find in blade and blossom
Sweet small voices odorous
Tender pleaders in my cause
That shall speak to me as I was
When the grass shall cover me.

Ah, beloved, in my sorrow
Very patient I can wait,
Knowing that, or soon or late,
There will be a clearer Morrow:
When your heart will moan: Alas!
Now I know how true she was;
Now I know how dear she was—
When the grass grows over me.

After leaving the Oakland city library Miss Coolbrith returned to San Francisco. For the next ten years she served as librarian for the Bohemian Club. She soon re-established her home there, and it became a gathering place for literary and cultured people of the city.

In 1881 Ina published her first book of verse, *A Perfect Day and Other Poems,* dedicated to her mother. Another volume of collected verse, *Songs from the Golden Gate,* was published in 1896. This latter book was dedicated to Edmund Clarence Stedman. It was a success and went into many editions. The last book of verse compiled by Miss Coolbrith, *Wings of the Sunset,* was published after her death by her niece, Mrs. Ina Cook. It is almost a collector's item today.

Ina Coolbrith was indeed an elect lady. Her life had been rich in many unusual experiences. Not only was she born at a pivotal point in the expansion and development of the West, but she was destined to play a star role in that fabulous pageant. For years the poetess had been writing and collecting material for a book on western literary history. She intended to include within it many valuable letters that she had received from such notables as the poetess Queen of Romania, Alfred Lord Tennyson, Robert Browning, George Meredith, the Rossettis, and other European writers. From her own United States were letters from Whittier, Longfellow, and many others. Some of these "greats" had been guests in her home.

By the spring of 1906 she had completed her huge task, and a publisher had accepted the manuscript. It was ready for mailing. On the evening of April 17, 1906 Ina Coolbrith retired with plans for the morrow just as all San Franciscans did. At 5:14 the next morning everyone was literally shaken from his bed by an unprecedented earthquake which was followed immediately by a devastating fire. The tragedy took Ina's unpublished manuscript and irreplaceable mementos; it also took her home and left her destitute. Yet she took her pen in hand and wrote a poem of hope for the city she loved:

SAN FRANCISCO

(April 18, 1906)

In olden days, a child I trod thy sands,
Thy sands unbuilded, rank with bush and briar
And blossom—chased the sea foam on thy strands—
Young City of my love and my desire.

I saw thy barren hills against the skies
I saw them topped with minaret and spire;
Wall upon wall their myriad mansions rise—
Fair City of my love and my desire.

From thee the Orient touched heart and hands,
The world wide argosies lay at thy feet
Queen of the queenliest land of lands
Our sunset glory, regal, glad, and sweet!

I saw thee in thine anguish tortured! prone!
Rent with earth-throes, garmented in fire
Each wound upon thy breast upon my own,
Sad City of my love and my desire.

Gray wind-blown ashes, broken toppling wall
And ruined hearth—are these thy funeral pyre?

Black desolation covering as a pall
Is this the end—my love and my desire?

Nay! strong, undaunted, thoughtless of despair,
The will that builded thee shall build again,
And all thy broken promises spring more fair,
Thou mighty mother of as mighty men.

Thou wilt arise invincible! Supreme!
The world to voice thy glory never tire;
And song unborn shall chant no nobler theme
Great City of my love and my desire.

But I will see thee ever as of old!
Thy wreath of pearl, wall, mineral, and spire,
Framed in the mists that veil the Golden Gate—
Lost City of my love and my desire.

Through her long life of love and service, Ina Coolbrith had made legions of friends. In her hour of distress and destitution many, many friends were anxious to repay her for her consideration and selfless service. They realized how difficult it would be for her to begin again, now that she was older and the "City of her love and desire" smoldered at her feet.

Letters of condolence and material considerations and gifts came from all over the world. Her California friends initiated projects to help her. Fellow-writers and literary-minded friends organized a group, "The Spinners," in her behalf. They compiled a book of short stories, poems, and articles. The volume was published by Paul Elder, a book man of San Francisco. This, and other undertakings, proved a success. A substantial amount of money was accumulated, and a home was bought for the beloved poetess. She lived here for many years, and the home became a mecca for the great and would-be great in San

Francisco's literary groups. Here the ambitious Ina initiated a phenomenal organization among world writers.

San Francisco did not grovel long in ashes and ruin. Like the Phoenix Bird, it arose in greater splendor from its ashes.

In 1915 San Francisco celebrated the completion of the Panama Canal by entertaining the world at that most glamorous of World Fairs, *The Panama, Pacific International Exposition.* Long before its opening, civic, commercial, industrial, religious, state, national and international organizations and men of wealth used their money and influence to bring conventions, cavalcades, and famous talent to San Francisco. Ina Coolbrith was now seventy years of age, in good health, had a vigorous mind, and was ambitious. She still twinkled, a bright star in the firmament of the New San Francisco.

Miss Coolbrith undertook the arduous task of organizing the *International Congress of Authors and Journalists.* All nations and groups, great and small, were contacted. "Every nation, kindred tongue and people" were invited to come to San Francisco and participate. There were lectures, conferences, readings, discussion, and symposiums dealing with every facet of the writer's art. Never did Ina Coolbrith demonstrate greater power of leadership and hard work. She wrote thousands of letters with her own hand and pen for four years. Each delegate felt at ease and able to contribute.

At the conclusion of the *International Congress of Authors and Journalists* on June 30, 1915, Ina Coolbrith was crowned with a wreath of California laurel. President Benjamin Ide Wheeler of the University of California placed the wreath on the head of the seventy-four-year-old woman. The legislature of the state passed a resolution declaring her "first poet laureate of the great state of California." For thirteen years she wore her crown with regal dignity—true Victorian that she was!

Ina Coolbrith attracted literary and artistic people like a magnet for half a century. In age, her friends gathered at the home of their beloved poetess on Broadway on the third Sunday afternoon. The stimulating ocean air tingled and flushed their cheeks as they climbed the hill. Miss Coolbrith, in a gown of dainty, pastel figures and a lace mantilla over her head which also lay in soft folds across her shoulders, greeted each with a firm handshake and sincere interest. There were spontaneity, wit, and fellowship, but never was there careless intimacy as some writers have inferred.

No matter how early guests arrived, Miss Coolbrith was dressed and ready to receive. The small group had organized themselves, and were known as The California Literary Society. Many came from a great distance. None appreciated Miss Coolbrith's soirees more than Dr. Bland, who had known many writers of the Golden Age. He was frequently referred to in his day as the link connecting the past and present in California writing. He published an account of Ina Coolbrith in the San Jose *Mercury-Herald* on March 9, 1928.

Dr. Bland was met by a barrage of questions when he met with his class in "Writers of the Pacific Coast" on the morning of March 9th. Groups were sitting with heads together and noses in the "Mercury."

"Is it true that Ina Coolbrith's real name is Smith?" "Why tell it after she's dead?" "Who 'wised' you up?"

Dr. Bland set his upper teeth on his lower lip, stood silent for a moment until all was quiet, then he began: "Last week, as you know, I attended our beloved Poet Laureate's funeral. I arrived at the place of service early. Another man was already there. I sat down at his side and began talking. I told him I had ridden forty miles to attend the service. He informed me that he had driven in from the San Joaquin Valley. I said, 'You must be most appreciative of Miss Coolbrith's poetry.'

" 'I am, she is also a relative, so I have a double interest in her,' he replied. I doubted this. Like others, I thought that Miss Coolbrith's niece at whose home she had died in Berkeley was the only living relative. No one had ever said it, it had just been accepted as a fact.

" 'I intend writing a biographical sketch of her life, perhaps you may be of service to me. Would you mind telling me how nearly you are related?' I asked.

" 'Not at all,' he replied. 'Miss Coolbrith's father and my grandfather were brothers, and that would make us. . . .' The music for the service began and further conversation was impossible. I asked the man for his name and address. A card was cheerfully passed. However, we did not meet again after the service."

The literary world in general, and California in particular, was thrown into a dither a few days after the death of Ina Coolbrith, when Robert Davis of the New York *Sun* cracked the story in his paper with a heavy headline. "Late Poet Laureate, Ina Coolbrith, Real Name Smith. Related to founder of Mormonism." The story was generally discredited, although Davis claimed he got his "scoop" from a man named Robert H. Smith. Eastern newspapers and writers contacted Western newspapers in San Francisco, home of the late Poet Laureate, requesting confirmation or denial. In the literary West, Dr. Henry Meade Bland was an accepted authority on history and writers of the Pacific Slope, as has been stated. His opinion was asked.

Dr. Bland continued his talk to his class: "After I received the call from San Francisco, I recalled meeting the man named Smith at the funeral, and I reasoned 'could be.' " His eyes twinkled as one who had just found a diamond in the dust. He went on to recount how he had called Smith, an engineer, at his project in the San Joaquin Valley. Mr. Smith had not seen the New York *Sun*, nor had he ever heard of Bob Davis, the reporter. However, he confirmed the story.

"The reporter is correct," said Dr. Bland. "Ina Coolbrith's real name is Josephine Donna Smith. She was the daughter of Don Carlos Smith, the Prophet's youngest brother, and Agnes Coolbrith Smith. She was named Donna for her father and Josephine for her grandfather, Joseph Smith, Sr. Joseph Smith, Jr., the Prophet, was her favorite uncle. Her father and her uncle were very close to each other, both were writers." Doctor Bland then went on to relate how intolerance and persecution had made the sincere but poverty-stricken Smiths a united family. When one suffered, all suffered.

When Pickett's covered wagon rumbled through Utah in 1852, Agnes Smith Pickett stopped long enough to visit Samuel Smith, son of Samuel H. Smith, her husband's brother, and her dearest friend, Mary Bailey Smith. If Agnes Coolbrith Smith Pickett visited other Smith relatives in the Territory, no known record is left. Samuel was fourteen years old at the time, and had related the incident to his son, J. Winter Smith, who was the engineer Dr. Bland had met at Ina Coolbrith's funeral. When Mr. Smith came to Stanford University at Palo Alto, he went to San Francisco and renewed the family friendship with the gracious Miss Coolbrith.

Following the earthquake and fire of 1906, the young Stanford student went immediately to the stricken city, and volunteered as a disaster relief worker. He was most concerned for the welfare of his father's poetess cousin. They had mutual respect and interest for each other. On one occasion Mr. Smith asked Miss Coolbrith, "Why have you never told your real name?"

"Long ago when my stepfather was establishing himself in business in the new state, my mother deemed it expedient to keep our name a secret. Prejudice against the Church was intense. Innuendo and inference could easily have injured his aspirations. Sister and I made the promise. Mother died without releasing us from that vow," said the poetess. Then she added thoughtfully, "To me a promise is a sacred thing."

"To me, also, a promise is a promise, and I promise to respect your confidence. Thanks for telling me, but how do you actually feel about your name?" asked Smith.

"When I am gone, you may tell the world," she replied.

Smith's giving of the facts to Dr. Bland for a press release was a fulfillment of her wishes.

The California Legislature adjourned the day of their beloved Poet Laureate's funeral. They also named a 7,900 foot mountain portaling Beckwourth Pass "Mount Ina Coolbrith."

Many years after Miss Coolbrith's death, Mr. Smith met reporter Bob Davis, who first gave the story of her real name in the New York *Sun* in March 1928. Mr. Davis remarked, "It's wonderful that the world knows who she is as well as what she is, a most extraordinary woman."

THE END

Notes, References, Sources

Bailey, Paul, *For This Is My Glory;* Westmoreland Press, 1940 (fiction).

Baker, Joseph E., *History of Alameda County;* Vol. 1, p. 356.

Bancroft, H. H., *Bancroft's Works;* San Francisco, 1890; Vol. XXII, p. 158; Vol. XXIII, p. 32.

Bancroft, H. H., *History of California;* History Publishing Co., San Francisco; Vol. V, pp. 469-472: Brannan's company arrives in California July 31, 1846; first non-Catholic church service; first newspaper; Chapters VI and VII. California beginnings, Chapter VIII.

Burnett, P. H., *Recollections and Observations of an Old Pioneer;* Appleton, N. Y. 1880; Chapter II, pp. 52 ff.,: Legal counsel for Joseph Smith at Liberty Jail 1838-39; chief counsel after Doniphan leaves case; pp. 56-63, prepares defense for Daviess County Grand Jury.

Cannon, George Q., *My First Mission;* Nibley H. Stevens, Salt Lake City, Utah, 1944; p. 185: John M. Horner receives printing press for publishing Book of Mormon in Hawaiian language.

Carter, Kate B. (compiler), *Heart Throbs of the West;* Self-published, Salt Lake City, 1949; Vol. I, II, X, p. 429: $4,280 tithing from California Mormons (1849).

Cowley, M. F., *Journal of Wilford Woodruff;* Deseret News, Salt Lake City, 1854; p. 356 recommended Stake (branch) at Horner ranch in California.

Driggs, Howard, *The Pony Express Goes Through;* Fred A. Stokes, N. Y. 1935.

Eager, John, *The Mormons in California;* unpub. manuscript at Bancroft Library, Univ. of Calif., Berkeley, Calif.

Evans, John H., *One Hundred Years of Mormonism;* Deseret Sunday School Union, Salt Lake City, 1909.

Fremont, John C., *Geographical Memoir;* Bigelow, N. Y., 1856; edited by Allen Nevin.

Gilbert, Col. F. T., *History of San Joaquin County;* Thompson and West, Oakland, Calif., 1879; p. 19: Mormons on the Stanislaus in 1846.

Halley, Wm., *Centennial Year Book* (A History of Alameda County); Oakland, Calif., 1876; p. 544: a history of Alameda County; pp. 461-467, biographical sketch of Thomas Eager; Brooklyn created and bounded, pp. 57 and 545.

Hall, Fredrick, *History of San Jose;* San Francisco, 1871; p. 223: Deseret petitions to become East California.

Higgins, F. Hal, Private collection of papers of John M. Horner; Walnut Creek, Calif. Uncopyright.

Hittell, Theodore H., *History of California;* Stone, San Francisco, 1897; Vol. II, pp. 593-595: Mormons land; first newspaper in San Francisco; first extra printed in state Oct. 1846, first regular edition Jan. 1847; pp. 663-694, 731 Mormons leave California; pp. 802-805, Deseret (Utah) requests amalgamation with California as East California.

History of Washington Township; published by Woman's Improvement Club, 1904; re-published Stanford Univ. Press, Stanford University, Palo Alto, California, 1950.

Horner, John M., *National Finance and Public Money;* Self-published, Honolulu, T.H., 1898.

Hunt, Rockwell D., *History of California;* Lewis, Chicago, 1926; p. 365: Alameda County.

Hoover, M. B., Rensch, H. E. and E. G., *Historic Spots in California;* Stanford Univ. Press, Stanford University, Palo Alto, Calif., 1932, 1933, 1934, and 1948.

Hunter, Milton R., *Brigham Young, Colonizer;* Zion Pub. Co., Independence, Mo., 1945.

Inman, Col. Henry C. and Cody, Wm. F., *The Great Salt Lake Trail;* Macmillan, London and N. Y., 1898; Chapter VI, pp. 101, 121, 126: Mormons adopt a scorched earth policy to stop Johnston's Army; burning of Ft. Bridger and Ft. Supply; suffering of U. S. soldiers.

Knowland, J. R., *California Landmarks;* Oakland *Tribune,* Oakland, Calif., 1941.

Lewis' (pub. co.) *Illustrated History of San Joaquin County.*

Manly, Wm. L., *Death Valley in '49;* Pacific Tree and Vine Co., San Jose, Calif., 1894; Chapter VIII, p. 74: Salt Lake Valley in 1849; emigrants pay guide in Mormon money; emigrants desert Hunt and are trapped in desert valley which they name "Death Valley." Hunt exonerated.

McGlashan, C. P., *History of the Donner Party;* Carlisle, San Francisco, 1879; p. 105: John Rhoads wades quagmire; p. 112, seven men to the rescue; Rhoads carries Naomi Pike over the Sierras; Rhoads monument at Slough House.

Merritt, F. C., *History of Alameda County;* Chicago, Illinois, 1928; p. 90; John W. Horner and Alameda County; first white American.

Peckham, Judge R. F., *An Eventful Life* (autobiographical); San Jose Pioneer, San Jose, Calif., 1897; only non-Mormon on New Hope Project; mounted clippings at Bancroft Library at the University of California, Berkeley, Calif.

Phillips, Catherine C., *Portsmouth Plaza, Cradle of San Francisco;* Nash, San Francisco, 1932; pp. 62-65: *Brooklyn* like Noah's Ark, landed at Yerba Buena July 31, 1846.

Pyper, Geo. D., *Stories of Latter-day Saints Hymns;* Deseret Sunday School Union, Salt Lake City, 1939; p. 28.

Scott, R. H. *Samuel Brannan and the Golden Fleece;* Macmillan, N.Y., 1944; Book II, pp. 59-182: voyage to Calif., Americanism in Calif., Book III, pp. 187-410, Brannan's meteoric rise to wealth, social, and political leadership; Book IV, pp. 413-442, Harper Library gift of I. M. Van Cott—first library in English in San Francisco (see Ch. III, p. 93).

Roberts, B. H., *Mormon Battalion, Its History and Achievements;* Deseret News, Salt Lake City, 1919.

Roberts, B. H., *Outlines of Ecclesiastical History;* Deseret News, Salt Lake; Chapter IX, p. 392.

Sherer, J. A. B., *Golden Tea Caddy;* Minton, Balch, N. Y., 1925

Sherman, W. T., *Memoirs;* Self-published, N. Y., 1875; p. 52: visits Mormon Island in 1848.

Smith, Hyrum M. and J. M. Sjodahl, *Doctrine and Covenants Commentary;* Deseret News, Salt Lake, 1923.

Smith, Ruby, *Mary Bailey;* Deseret News, Salt Lake, 1954; Chapter XXII, p. 105: Temple ordinances done by Agnes Coolbrith before leaving for St. Louis.

Stewart, Geo., *Ordeal by Hunger;* Henry Holt, N. Y., 1936; Chapter XX, pp. 177-195.

Stookey, Dr. Walter, *Fatal Decisions;* Deseret News, Salt Lake, 1950.

Tinkham, Geo. H., *History of Stanislaus County;* Historic Records Pub. Co. Los Angeles, 1921; p. 41: Mormon first settlement on the Stanislaus in 1846.

Tinkham, Geo. H., *History of San Joaquin County;* Historic Records Publishing Co., Los Angeles, 1921.

Thompson and West, *Historical Atlas of Alameda County;* Published by authors, 1878; p. 22: Thomas Eager introduces resolution combining San Antonio, Clinton, and other territory into Brooklyn in honor of ship which brought first Americans by water in 1846. Maps of Brooklyn and Washington Townships.

Walker, Dr. Franklin, *San Francisco's Literary Frontiers;* Alfred A. Knopf, N.Y., 1943; much heretofore unprinted material on Ina Coolbrith (Josephine Donna Smith).   (For Miss Coolbrith's marriage see *Los Angeles County Marriage Certificates,* Vol. I, p. 22-23.   For her divorce see *Los Angeles County District Court,* Case 853, Josephine D. Carsley vs. Robert B. Carsley, granted December 30, 1861.)   Pickett saves Ina Coolbrith from physical harm by wounding Carsley. (See Los Angeles *Star,* Oct. 19, 1861.) *Wings of Sunset* dedicated to the "boy Carl."

Wood, W. M., *History of Alemada County;* Self-published, Oakland, Calif., 1883; p. 417: Brooklyn named for Mormon ship.

Wentworth, May, *Poetry of the Pacific;* Pacific Publishing Co., San Francisco, 1867; pp. 343-345. (Coolbrith Poems) Thought to be autobiographical.

NEWSPAPERS, MAGAZINES, AND LETTERS

NEWSPAPERS

Berkeley *Daily Gazette*, Berkeley, California: Johnson, "Monuments to Mormons," Oct. 20, 1949.

California Farmer, San Francisco, Calif.; from F. H. Higgin's private file. Uncopyright.

California Star, San Francisco, Calif.; photostat file at the California State Library, Sacramento, Calif.

California Star, bound volumes; Vol. I, Bancroft Library.

Deseret News, Salt Lake City; bound file Huntington Library.
   Sept. 25, 1854, Horner's dept. store at Tithing Office.
   Jan. 20, 1955, Horner's dept. store at Tithing Office.
   March issues, 1855, Young thanks Horner.
   April 6, 1918, article by Austin, "The Brooklyn."

Improvement Era:
   July 1936, Story of Samuel Brannan.
   May through Sept. 1904, Autobiographical story of John M. Horner.
   Jan. 1950, Ina Coolbrith (Josephine Donna Smith).
   1902 (a serial), Story of Joseph Smith (Salisbury).

Messenger:
   July and Aug. 1950; Dec. 1950; Mar. 1953; Sept. 1957; articles by A. D. Patton.

Oakland *Tribune*, Oakland, California:
   Dec. 23, 1951, Washington Township.
   June 3, 1956, L. Verborg.
   Apr. 18, 1954, Samuel's History of Post Offices.
   May 6, 1954, Return to Donner Lake.
   May 4, 1952, Stormy events in the history of Oakland Library.
   Articles by A. D. Patton Aug. 13, 20, 1950; May 11, 18, 25, and June 8, 1951; Jan. 28, Feb. 4, 11, 18, 1952; and April 28, 1957.

Sacramenta *Union*, Sacramento, California:
   Sept. 11, 1866.

San Jose *Mercury Herald*, San Jose, California:
   Mar. 9, 1928, articles by Dr. Henry Meade Bland.

San Jose *Pioneer*, San Jose, California:
   June 16-23, 1877, biography of Judge Peckham.

Scoop, San Francisco, California, 1954; pp. 55-60.

Scott, R. H., *Westvaco Digest*, Mar. 1942; "Gold to Magnesium."

Sun:
   San Bernardino *Sun*, San Bernardino, Calif., June 26, 1932.
   New York *Sun*, Mar. 6, 1928.

Touring Topics:
   Apr. 1930, W. B. Houston.

LETTERS

Oakland Public Libarry scrapbook of letters from 1890-1893.

Oakland Public Library letters of Green of 1923-1925.

Mabel Thomas' (Oakland librarian) letter to John McLaughlin of Brooklyn, N.Y. concerning the ship, *Brooklyn,* being the origin of the name, Brooklyn Town, in Alameda County.

John M. Horner's undated letter to his children in the Higgin's collection. The original is owned by Edna Horner Matthisen of Santa Cruz, Calif.

Ella C. Cummings' letter to Carlton Kendall, March 12, 1928; Huntington Library.

Correspondence of the Author:

Letters to the California Centennial Commission 1948, 1949, 1950. Letters to and from the San Francisco, Sacramento, San Diego, and San Bernardino Chambers of Commerce. Other correspondence with the Ventura Public Library; Kate B. Carter, Pres. Daughters of Utah Pioneers, Salt Lake City; Frances Larson, Sec. *Grizzly Bear,* Anaheim, Calif., Mar. 1954; Liberty Parlor, Native Daughters of Golden West, Elk Grove, Calif.; Earl Olson, L.D.S. Church Historian's Office, Salt Lake City, Utah; David W. Cummings, Honolulu, T. H.; J. Winter Smith, San Jose, Calif.; Clara Barton, Landmark Chairman, San Bernardino, Calif.

MAGAZINES, PERIODICALS, PAMPHLETS

California Historical Quarterly, Everett, A., Sept. 1958.

Spirit, Catholic Magazine.

Carter, Kate B. (Compiler), *Journal of Henry Bigler, Journal of John Borrowman, Journal of John Eager, Journal of Nathaniel V. Jones, Mormons in California;* Daughters of Utah Pioneers.

This Is San Diego, San Diego Chamber of Commerce.

San Bernardino, San Bernardino Chamber of Commerce.

BROCHURES

Place Names in California, American Trust Co., Calif., 1954.

Street Names in California, American Trust Co., Calif., 1954.

Romney, Thomas, *Gospel in Action;* an account of John C. Neagle (Naile).

MANUSCRIPTS

Eager, John, Bancroft Library, Berkeley, California.

Bigler, Henry, Bancroft Library, Berkeley, California, Mss. No. 60.

Glover, William, Bancroft Library, Berkeley, California.
Horner, John M., Higgins collection, Walnut Creek, Calif.
Hunter, Jane E., De Young Museum, San Francisco
Jones, Mary E., Bancroft Library, Berkeley, California.
Rhoads, John, Bancroft Library, Berkeley, California.
Richards, F. D., Bancroft Library, Berkeley, California.
Stanley, R. H. Scott, excerpts from the *Journal of Parley P. Pratt.*
    Tells of Horner giving $2,000 for San Bernardino Colony.

PICTURES AND PHOTOGRAPHS

California Society of Pioneers, San Francisco, California.
Berkeley Stake Messenger.
Photographer Edward A. Pyle.
Photographer Alma Scheuller.
California State Library, Sacramento, Calif.

SUPPLEMENTARY INFORMATION

A. Early Mormon Activities in California.
B. *Brooklyn* passengers—Active Members, 1857.
C. Mormon Landmarks on Historic Sites in California.
    Fort Hill, Los Angeles, Calif. incomplete as of this date.
D. Mormon Names in Early California.

EARLY MORMON ACTIVITIES IN CALIFORNIA

The early California Mormons were zealous church workers. After the discovery of gold in California and before the "gold rush" Jefferson Hunt opened the first road over the Sierra Nevadas as faithful Battalion men and some *Brooklyn* Saints went to the central gathering place established in the Salt Lake Valley a year earlier (1847).

One week after the arrival at Yerba Buena (San Francisco) July 31, 1846, regular church services began at the home of Samuel Brannan. He had rented the largest house in the hamlet, vacant home of Captain Richardson, collector of the port. (Port Master.) This is said to be the first religious service held in San Francisco. The Mission Delores was separate from Yerba Buena. The local church members were loyal. In Sept. 1849, $4,280.00 tithing was sent to church headquarters by the California members, in addition to personal contributions. Proselyting began early.

John M. Horner, an elder, held cottage meetings in what became Alameda County as early as 1848. Some time in late 1848 or 1849 regular church services were held in the Naile (old Mormon adobe) on the Michael Overaker place near Niles, Alameda Co.

Scott, quotes eleven members in addition to Brannan as apostatized, or were disfellowshipped in the early years. This would be little above average of general church membership. The Church had only been organized 16 years in 1846, and had grown very rapidly.

Muir, Leo, says of Ghost Branches in California, "Parley P. Pratt succeeded Samuel Brannan as leader and officially excommunicated him, however, Glover, Sparks and others officiated after Brannan's apostasy and excommunication.

Ghost Branches:

Buckeye Branch, Yolo County, organized December 31, 1856.
    Hezakiah Thatcher, presiding elder. Eleven members.
    Elders Henry G. Boyle, David M. Stewart, and William H. Sherman, laboring missionaries in area.
Dry Creek Branch, near Petaluma, organized March 10, 1857.
    Elder Boyle, formerly of Mormon Battalion officiating. 20 members.
Salinas Branch (Pajaro, Santa Cruz conference) organized April 1857. Twenty-one members, Curtis Stiles President. (Many members went to San Bernardino later.)
Dry Town, Amador County, branch organized May 17, 1857.
    Thomas Hinley president. This branch resulted from missionary labors of Elders Fred W., and Charles C. Hurst.
Santa Clara, Branch, Santa Clara County, early in 1854—largely through missionary efforts of Elder William McBride.
Centerville—Niles, Elder John M. Horner held cottage meetings soon after other church members came to Southern Alameda Co., in 1848. History of Washington Township says "Horner preached to a congregation of about forty members at his school house in 1850." Made a presiding elder in 1851—because it was near Mission San Jose (Catholic) the branch is sometimes referred to as *San Jose Branch.* On October 6, 1853 Conference was held in San Bernardino, and again sustained John M. Horner president of San Jose Branch—Muir.
    Wilford Woodruff Journal (Published by M. F. Cowley, 1909) chapter 32, page 356, records the general church conference announcing advisability of organizing "A stake" at the Horner Ranch in California.

BROOKLYN PASSENGERS—ACTIVE MEMBERS AS OF 1857

All journals and diaries were lost, even the day-to-day journal of Caroline A. Joyce. Mrs. Joyce kept a daily record of the voyage, also a record of the happenings after the landing and the impact of the gold rush (1849) which peopled California with every race, creed, color and stratum of society in such numbers as to be granted statehood within a year. This priceless manuscript disappeared shortly before or at the time of the author's death in San Francisco.

When Hubert H. Bancroft began his voluminous writing of Western History he compiled, to the best of his sources a list of the *Brooklyn's* passengers. He used a list of those who registered while at Honolulu and from the memory of living fellow passengers. Subsequent history shows that some names were omitted. For this book (Pacific Pilgrims) I shall list the names alphabetically.

Addison, Isaac, and daughter. Returned to East Coast, left Church.
Aldrich, Silas, (died at sea) wife Prudence, son Josper and daughter. Later went to Bountiful, Utah.
Austin, Julius, wife and three children. Migrated to Laketown, Utah, eventually settled in the Bear Lake Country—Northern Utah.
Brannan, Samuel, wife and one son. Did not remain a church member, later excommunicated, exploited his brethren at Mormon Island. Became California's first millionaire, first citizen in that he donated land for California's first schoolhouse; built first Cliff House, first to introduce sheep, and wine grapes into Napa County. He helped organize First Historical Society, Academy of Science. Vigilance Committee, first railroad from Calistogo to Vallejo, also from Sacramento to Yuba, first real estate promoter, first newspaper publisher in San Francisco, and many other firsts. Died in poverty.
Church Members, as of 1857 Record—Scott
Buckland, Alondis L. D. (and Mother—) Buckland stayed at "New Hope" on the Stanislaus until the last. He built the first big hotel in San Francisco—was in business there for a long time, later went to Bountiful, Utah.
Bullen, Newel, wife and three children. Went to Richmond, Utah.
Burr, Charles O., wife and child. Carpenter, built one of the first Mormon homes in San Francisco. Later migrated to Burrville, Utah. Bought one of the sawmills brought on the *Brooklyn.*
Burr, Nathan and wife—No record.
Cade, (or Kincaid) and wife—said to have freighted on the prairies with John R. Robbins. (See Muir.)—lived in Utah.
Clark, Sophia P. (later King) lived in San Francisco, and in Utah for a short time, but most of her life in Alameda, California, where she died January 8, 1909. At the time claimed to be the last survivor. This is disputed.
Clark, William S. (Sophia's brother) built Long Wharf—Clark's point, named for him. Hittell says Vol. IV page 595 in *History of California.* In July 1848 while Governor Mason was at Mormon Island mines, William Clark asked "Governor, what business has Sam Brannan to collect tithes from us here?" Mason answered, "Brannan has a perfect right to collect from you Mormons as long as you Mormons are D-- fools enough to pay them" (the tithes.) Brannan never collected another cent. Clark is not on Bancroft's list.

Coombs, Abraham, wife, two daughters, a son and some grand-
children.   Resided in San Francisco and at Redwood Canyon
(near Oakland) where he had a sawmill, went to San Bernardino, from there started to Utah in 1858, died at Beaver, Utah.
He had four children while living in California.   His widow
taught school in Cedar City, Utah, died there in 1863.

Corwin, Fanny M.—Mother-in-law of Samuel Brannan remained a
devout L.D.S.   Died and was buried in San Francisco in the
1850's (Scott.)

Eager, John, Printer on first San Francisco Newspaper (*California
Star*).   Went to Utah when Jefferson Hunt opened Emigrant
Carson Road 1848.   Later lived in Arizona.

Eager, Thomas, Oakland businessman, and politician. Had East
Oakland named Brooklyn.   Long served as sergeant at arms
in California Assembly.   Lived in Santa Cruz.

Ex*Eager*, Lucy, Excommunicated at sea by Brannan. Later married
an army man.   Was a greatly misrepresented woman.   No record of daughters.

Ensighn, Elias, (died at sea, also a daughter).
*Widow—no record: son went to Utah.   Mrs. James Richard-
son of ElCerito, California is a descendant.

Evans, William, wife and four children.   Evans first tailor in San
Francisco—shop at what later became Market and Van Ness
Streets.   Later migrated to Centerville, Utah.   Granddaughter
Hilda Evans Perkins former stake president in Oakland Relief
Society.

Fisher, Joseph R. and wife Mary Ann.   Mary Ann Fisher buried
at old Oak Hill Cemetery San Jose, California.

Fowler, Jerusha and four children. Stayed in California.

Glover, William, wife and three children. Counselor to Brannan,
carried on after Brannan left church, until re-organization, did
carpenter work on California's first schoolhouse (Brannan
donated lot).   Took $4,280 tithing from California to Church
headquarters at Salt Lake, Sept. 29, 1849. $3,000 was unminted.
See Carter, K., *Heart Throbs of West*, Vol. 10, page 429.) Lived
at Centerville, Utah.   Glover was member of first city council
of San Francisco.   (See *California Star*, Vol. 1.)

Goodwin, Isaac, wife Laura and seven children.   Wife died, was
buried at Juan Fernandez Islands on same Island where Alexander Selkirk (the real Robinson Crusoe) was put ashore and
awaited rescue.   Isaac Goodwin waded from the *Brooklyn* to
the plaza with Baby Albert in his arms.   He went to Mission
Delores to live, then to Centerville (or what was to become
Centerville, Alameda Co., Calif.)   His children's names are

*This territory was known as Brooklyn township.   Brooklyn (East Oak-
land) is older than the city of Oakland.   East Bay Inter State Center and
proposed Mormon Temple in Brooklyn Township.

recorded in the old Horner School, before Alameda County was created. Later they moved to San Bernardino, then to Southern Utah. Some sons married into aristocratic California families. Some entered into newspaper work.

Griffith, Johnathan, wife and two children. Lived in Calif.

Hamilton, Mary, two children. Died at San Bernardino.

Haskell, A. G. and wife.

Hayes, Jacob. Lived in California.

Hicks, Joseph. Stayed in California.

Horner, John Meir and wife. The Horners came to the "East Bay" almost immediately after landing from the *Brooklyn*, to share crop for Dr. John Marsh; came to what was to become Alameda Co., in March of 1847. First white American in county, became wealthy raising grain and potatoes and truck garden produce. Fed starving '49ers. He gave Alameda its first schoolhouse and non-Catholic meetinghouse; non-Catholic cemetery, first roads, fences, bridges, blacksmith shop and wheelright shop; first steamboat on San Francisco Bay, first steam driven flour mill, first combined harvester (with Beard). He founded many of the eight towns in Washington Township, was first presiding elder of Latter-day Saints Church in Alameda Co., read first marriage ceremony in Niles, was associated with George Q. Cannon in publishing Book of Mormon in Hawaiian language. He befriended stranded Mormon missionaries when leaving or returning from their fields through the port of San Francisco. On one occasion he contributed $5,500.00 in one donation. He helped pay for San Bernardino. He had eight children all born in Alameda County. He won the title of "First Farmer of California" at the first State Fair (1852). He maintained an early department store in Salt Lake City in the old Tithing Office Building.

He entered into business in the Hawaiian Islands where he passed away in 1907 at the age of 86.

Hyatt, Elisha, wife and son. No record.

Ira (*Irea*), Cyrus, among first miners to work at *Mormon Island*. Lived in California.

Joyce, John, wife Caroline and daughter. Remained in San Francisco. The Joyces were divorced. John Joyce was excommunicated. Family remained in the church. Mrs. Joyce later married Col. Jackson. She wrote the most complete journal of the voyage of the *Brooklyn* and early life of the Church in San Francisco—which was lost shortly before her death. The Joyces first lived in a little house on the edge of the village (now said to have been near Jackson and Taylor streets) during the winter of 1846-47. A surgeon of the U. S. Sloop of War *Warren* which was anchored in San Francisco Bay established the first "sanitorium" in San Francisco where he brought desperately sick men. Powell Street where the cable cars are now was first named for him. The steward at Dr. Powell's Sanitorium gave the Joyces (smuggled from the mess supplies) a quart of beans and pound salt pork for their Christmas dinner. Dr. Powell presented the Joyces with a slice of ham, a lump of butter (the size of a walnut) and a drawing of tea, and told Mr. Joyce where he could buy flour. There were no stoves in Yerba Buena that first Christmas (1846). However, Mrs. Joyce baked a cake between two pie tins in the ashes of the campfire in front of the old adobe, and invited Mrs. Robbins to share the repast. The Joyces' daughter became a writer. Augusta Joyce Crockson in Utah. Col. Jackson with his wife and stepdaughter lived for a while in San Bernardino before going to Utah.

Jones, Isabella (Mrs) remained in California.

Kemble, Edward C., Printer of first *California Star*, later mined gold—published first paper in Placerville (Hangtown).

Kittleman, Elizabeth, said to be a daughter of William, married Henry Dalton of the Mormon Battalion and later moved to Davis Co., Utah. Sarah Kittleman married Dr. E. P. Jones and moved to Ky.

Kittleman, John, wife Sarah, sons Thomas, and William, wife and six children. Thomas Kittleman married Angelina Lovett "a twenty-one-year-old spinster" who also came on *Brooklyn*. Ceremony performed by Elder Samuel Brannan, Dec. 19, 1847 (see bound vol. *California Star*, page 3, column 3). Said to be last official ecclesiastical function of Elder Brannan before his apostasy and subsequent excommunication. William Kittleman later lived in Salt Lake City, Utah.

Knowles, Richard, and wife. Salt Lake Valley, Utah.

Ladd, Samuel, lived in California under name Johnson, moved to St. George, Utah.

Lane, Emmeline A., died in California.

Leigh, Isaac, and wife, lived in Nevada.

Light, James, wife and child. Light began sharecropping at Marsh's landing with John M. Horner. May possibly have gone into the San Joaquin Valley after mining.

Lovett, Angelina, taught first English speaking school in California in an outbuilding at Mission Dolores (now San Francisco) shortly after the landing of the *Brooklyn*, possibly August 1846. Later married Thomas Kittleman.

MaCue, Patrick, wife and four children. Stayed in California.

Marshall, Earl, wife and family. The Marshalls settled in Southern Alameda County where Marshall operated first dairy, became a farmer. Descendant still in Alameda Co.

Meder, Moses A., wife Sarah and four children.

Mory, Barton, wife and two sons, Centerville, California.

Mory, Origin, and family. Centerville, California.

Mory, Rinaldo, and mother, Kaysville, Utah. The Moreys or

Morys were boat builders in early California. John Borrowman of the Mormon Battalion records under date May 13, 1848, of going from San Francisco to Sutters Fort (Sacramento) on "Mory's Launch." (Carter, Kate B. pamphlet—March of Mormon Battalion, Oct., 1945) Other Battalion men worked for the Morys. After the gold rush days the Morys settled in southern Alameda Co., "Mory's Road" and "Mory's Landing" and "Mory's School," are all named for them. Barton and Origin Mory are buried in the old Irvington Cemetery near the Stacy Horner lot. Many Morys in California now.

Moses, Ambrose T., Moses was disfellowshiped, his widow later moved to Salt Lake Valley, Utah, and took daughter Clarisa. One daughter, Ann Francis Moses married Eustaquco Valencia. Tradition says Valencia Street in San Francisco was named for this family. Ann Francis Valencia was first non-Catholic buried at Mission Delores (S. F.). Their genealogy stems down through the line of Lydia Valencia Hardy of Santa Rosa, California and through the Frederick Hatt Families of Berkeley, California.

Murray, Miss Mary, remained in California.

Narrimore, Edwin, (died at sea).

Narrimore, Mercy and child remained in Honolulu. No other record.

Nichols, Joseph, wife Jerusha and child early settled in southern Alameda Co. He became an agriculturist. Many descendants.

Nutting, Lucy, went to Lehi, Utah.

Oakley, Howard, Volunteered to help rescue the Donner Party Mar., 1847. Was not needed. Mined. Tradition says Oakley in Contra Costa County, California, is named for him. (This cannot be proved nor disproved.)

Pell, E. Ward. Pell, under name of Elijah W. Pell, sheriff of San Francisco, (See *California Star*) bound Vol. One, Bancroft Library, Berkeley, Calif. Pell was excommunicated at sea by Brannan. Many descendants in Alameda Co., or Contra Costa County. Early sheriff of San Francisco.

Petch, Robert, wife and two children. Remained in California.

Phillips, John, went to Beaver, Utah.

Poole, Peter, Mary, Elizabeth. Smithfield, Utah.

Read, Christina, John, Rachel and Hannah (Read) Jimison and child. In his diary John Borrowman, company B., Mormon Battalion, records under date of December 2, 1847, taking cloth to "Sister Reid" to make two garments after he had left some material with a woman to make him some shirts. He was in San Francisco at the time. He also records working for "Brother Clark." Reads went to Cache Valley, Utah.

Robbins, Isaac, wife and two children. Established first trucking and express business in San Francisco. His brothers were copartners in the one horse wagon venture, later moved to Provo, Utah.

Robbins, Charles, worked as a printed on the *California Star.* Joined his brothers and went back to New Jersey by way of Panama. Came to Utah in 1858 from Atlantic coast by mule team.

Robbins, John R., wife, and two children, became very wealthy— San Francisco real estate, including the site where the Palace Hotel was built in later years. With his brothers Charles, Isaac, and families, they all went by way of water and the Isthmus to the eastern coast; engaged in freighting by mule team between the Missouri and Salt Lake City. The John R. Robbins were parents of Georgiana *Pacific* Robbins. The child born aboard the *Brooklyn* between Honolulu and San Francisco. Later lived in Salt Lake City, Utah.

Rollins, Henry Isaac and daughter. No record.

Savage, Eliza. Moved to Salt Lake Valley, Utah. Married Truman Angell.

Scott, James. Salt Lake Valley, Utah, left Church.

Surrine, George. (See note 9 in reference.) (Surrine Saw)

Surrine, John, wife and child. The Surrines worked in the mines. Went to San Bernardino, San Diego, Arizona, and Paris, Idaho. (See Surrine Saw at Information Bureau on Temple Square, Salt Lake City.)

Skinner, Horace A., wife and child. No record.

Smith, Amelia, went to Salt Lake Valley, Utah.

Smith, Orin, wife and six children.

Smith, Robert, wife and two children. Sandy, Utah.

Snow, Zelnora. (See Glover), went to Farmington, Utah.

Sparks, Mary and family. No record.

Ex *Sparks,* Quartus S., *wife and *child. Quartus Sparks worked at New Hope, lived at Mission Delores; mined at Mormon Island, presided over San Francisco Branch temporarily. And was renowned as an eloquent speaker; moved to San Bernardino. Later left the Church. He was a lawyer.

Stark, Daniel, wife three children and foster child lived for a while in southern Alameda Co. Later moved to Payson, Utah.

Still, George, wife and three children. Stayed in California.

Stivers, Simon, stepson or adopted son of Earl Marshal. He married and lived in Niles, southern Alameda County, California, has many descendants in this area. "Stivers Pond" is named for him.

Stout, William, wife and child. Stout was foreman for founding colony at New Hope (1846). Brannan quarreled with him in spring of 1847 and discharged him as foreman. Stout quit, went to Santa Cruz where he later went into the lumber business.

Stringfellow, Jesse A., lived in San Jose, California.

Tompkins, Thomas; wife and two children established himself in
southern Alameda Co., (see Carter, K. B. Daughters of Utah
Pioneers pamphlet. Journal, Louise B. Pratt, April, 1947.)

Ward, Frank (non-member), was not a member of the Church.
No record.

Wimer, George K., wife and six children. Said to have descendants in Oakland, California. Sometimes spelled Winner.

Of the names listed in *Times and Seasons,* viz. Dan S. Baldwin,
Menena Cannon, Jonas Cook, James Embly, J. M. Farnsworth, Wil-
liam Flint, Joseph France, John Haibraid, William Mack, Stephen
H. Pierce, William Reamer, Dan Richardson, Charles Russell, Susan
A. Searls; Sam Smith, Simeon Stanley, ... Ferguson and
.... Maguire, I have no record of except *William H. Mack*
and also a *Marston* who was the teacher of the first school in
California, recorded by some as having come on the *Brooklyn.*
Mack lived in Southern Alameda Co., has descendant there. Lived
in San Francisco, and became a river pilot on the Sacramento River.

Elizabeth Bird, Howell of Clifton (or Preston) Idaho last
female survivor of *Brooklyn* came to San Francisco by air in 1940—
when bronze tablet was dedicated to landing of the *Brooklyn.*
She was 95 years old. She was an infant brought by Daniel Stark
family.

Albert Goodwin (father of Nancy Goodwin Baker) was last
male survivor.

MORMON LANDMARKS ON HISTORIC SITES
IN CALIFORNIA

Landmarks	Marked by
Tragedy Springs Massacre, Jackson-Silver Creek Highway, El Dorado Co. Three Mormon Battalion scouts killed by Indian June 22, 1848. Names carved on tree. Carving on tree later put in Sutter Fort Museum at Sacramento.	Temporary marker by Native Sons of Golden West. 1921.
Mormon Battalion Monument, placed by Daughters of Utah Pioneers and W.P.A. Art Project. Dedicated at San Diego, California, January 28, 1940.	W.P.A. Art Project and D.U.P. of San Diego.
Landing of Mormon Chartered Ship *Brooklyn* at San Francisco, Calif. July 31, 1946. Marker placed Aug. 4, 1940, at Broadway and Battery Streets (Daughters of Utah Pioneers, No. 60.)	San Francisco D.U.P.

Mormon Springs Road, San Bernardino Co., built in 1851 to establish mill to saw lumber for their homes. Mormon built road to first water dedicated Sept. 9, 1935.

Arrowhead Parlor N.S.G.W.

Mormon Council House—First Public Building in San Bernardino, Calif., built in 1852 on County Courthouse grounds, San Bernardino, Calif., dedicated June 25, 1932.

Lugonia Parlor 241 N.D.G.W.

Landmarks

Marked by

Fort Benson, created 1856 over Mormon and non-Mormon ownership sides were drawn on location not on religious lineup. Many Mormons on land of non-Mormons; many non-Mormons on Mormon-owned land. It never functioned as a military unit.

Dedicated by N.S.G.W. Arrowhead Parlor and Lugonia Parlor N.D.G.W.

Mormon Road (San Bernardino Co.) constructed by Mormon colonists to establish a sawmill, later known as Seeley Flats. Road built by men and teams in very short time up steep mountain side. Marked May 15, 1937.

N.S.G.W. Arrowhead No. San Bernardino

Pioneer Monument Marking Mormon Trail, High-gear road near Crestline, Calif. Erected and dedicated by Thursday Club, Crest Forest District, Nov. 10, 1932.

Thursday Club Crest Forest district.

Site of old Mormon adobe, on Michael Overaker home near Niles. Here Mormons held day school, social gatherings, and religious gatherings before 1850, built by John Conrad Naile, also spelled Neagle, sold to Overaker's father in 1854.

Not marked.

Pioneer Schoolhouse chapel approximately one mile from present Centerville chapel. Built by John M. Horner in Centerville in 1850. First non-Catholic church in Alameda County.

Alameda County camp Daughters of Utah Pioneers. Oct. 25, 1959

Landmarks

Marked by

Carson Emigrant Road first road out of California to Salt Lake Valley, 1848. Jefferson Hunt leader. Forty niners came into California over this road to the gold fields in 1848.

Not marked.

The Launch *Comet*—First sail launch to ascend San Joaquin River from San Francisco in autumn of 1846. Carried twenty Mormon pioneers to New Hope agriculture project at confluence of Stanislaus and San Joaquin Rivers. Later Doak and Bousell established first ferry on San Joaquin River at this site. State registered landmark No. 437. Tablet placed by California Centennial Commission—base furnished by Alameda County, Camp Daughters of Utah Pioneers. Dedicated Oct. 22, 1949.

California centennial commission, Oct. 22, 1949

Mormon Island, Sacramento, Calif. Site of second gold strike made by three ex-Mormon Battalion soldiers in late Jan., 1848.

Daughters of Utah Pioneers, Sept. 14, 1957

Landmarks

Marked by

Tablet placed by Sacramento County camps Daughters of Utah Pioneers.

Grave of John Rhoads, member of first Donner Relief Party, carried child Naomi Pike (later Mrs. Schenck) over snow-capped Sierra from Donner Lake to Johnson Ranch (near Marysville, Calif.) Marker placed at his grave, Slough House, Sacramento Co.

Liberty Parlor N.D.G.W. No. 213

Hon. Thomas Eager founder of Brooklyn (East Oakland).

Not marked

New Hope—1846—First Wheat Mormon Colony—First wheat in San Joaquin Valley, also other crops irrigated by pole and bucket method. Erected three log houses sawmill, ferry across Stanislaus River. Later known as Stanislaus City State Registered Landmark No. 436, base furnished by Alameda County Camp, Daughters of Utah Pioneers. Dedicated Oct. 22, 1949.

California Centennial Commission, and Alameda County, Daughters of Utah Pioneers, Oct. 22, 1949

Mormon monuments at Sycamore Grove; Honors Mormons who camped here 1851, negotiating purchasing land, later they established San Bernardino, unveiled June 1, 1927. Later destroyed by vandals.

Fred Klien Chicago publisher.

Landmarks

Marked by

Old Vallecito Stage Station on Butterfield

Marked by Mr.

Overland Mail Route. Presented to San Diego Co., Calif. Established 1846—a few months later the famed Mormon Battalion under Col. P. St. George Cook got first flour on their march from Fort Leavenworth (Kansas) to San Diego. (See: Knowland, J. R. Historic Landmarks.)

Charles F. Holland

Rubidoux grist mill. State registered landmark; built in 1846-1847 furnished flour to Mormon Battalion on their trek to San Diego, 1847

Registered landmark by state Oct. 1931

El Adobe de los Robles Rancho near Lemoore. Home of Daniel Rhoads, Mormon boy (youngest in party) who rescued Donner Party in 1847. Now county museum.

Marked by Kings County Museum

Hope Valley named by Mormon opening up Carson Emigrant trail when they reached summit of Sierra Nevadas.

Not marked

Pleasant Valley, Ed Dorado Co., (Near present site of Placerville, rendezvous of the Mormons leaving for Salt Lake Valley left June 21, 1848. About fifty men and one woman. Not far away was a place where these Mormons built wagons and bought horses for trip. Was called *Mormon Corral*.

Not marked

Landmarks

Marked by

Mormon well—San Diego Co., where Mormon Battalion men dug for coal in 1847.

Not marked

Mt. Joseph Smith once name of Mt. Palomar. See American Trust Co. brochure, 1954.

Not marked

MORMON NAMES IN EARLY CALIFORNIA

1846 - 1851—First five years of United States Occupation

Mormon Island—Sacramento Co., California. Second gold strike.
Mormon Gulch—Toulumne Co., California (Later Tuttle town).
Mormon Road—Toulumne Co., California. Slungullion Rd.
Mormon Bar—Mariposa Co., California.
Mormon Corral—El Dorado Co., California, gathered stock for Emigrant Road, 1848.
Mormon Springs—San Bernardino Co., California.

Mormon Road—San Bernardino Co., California, now Crestline Road.
Mormon Channel—San Joaquin Co., California, near Stockton.
Mormon Well—San Diego Co., California. Old Coal Mine.

GEOGRAPHIC NAMES ASSOCIATED WITH OR NAMED BY EARLY MORMONS

Tragedy Spring—El Dorado Co., Mormon Battalion killed by Indians, 1848.
New Hope—San Joaquin Co., first wheat in valley, 1846.
Comets Landing—San Joaquin Co., First Ferry, 1846.
Horner Schoolhouse chapel—Alameda Co., First non-Catholic chapel.
Clarks Point—First long Wharf—San Francisco Co.
Pleasant Valley—El Dorado Co. Rendezvous of Mormons who opened Emigrant Carson Road, 1848.
First Schoolhouse—San Francisco, California, 1847.
Hope Valley—Alpine County—Emigrant-Carson Road, 1848.
Mt. Smith—San Diego County, now Mt. Palomar.
Genoa Nev. Then a part of Utah—Emigrant Carson Road, 1848, Later, Mormon Station, 1851.

Index